WOMEN of SMOKE

WOMEN of SMOKE

Latin American Women in Literature & Life

MARJORIE AGOSIN

Translated by Janice Molloy

The Red Sea Press, Inc.
Publishers & Distributors of Third World Books
556 Bellevue Avenue
Trenton, New Jersey 08618
(609) 695-3402

The Red Sea Press, Inc.
556 Bellevue Avenue
Trenton, New Jersey 08618

First American Edition 1989

Library of Congress Catalog Card Number: 88-63387

ISBN: 0-932415-42-3 Cloth
       0-932415-43-1 Paper

PRINTED AND BOUND IN CANADA

Acknowledgements

"The General's Bonfires: The Death of Rodrigo Rojas in Chile" was previously published in *Human Rights Quarterly 9*, Fall 1987.

"A Visit to the Mothers of the Plaza de Mayo" was previously published in *Human Rights Quarterly 9*, Fall 1987.

"Metaphors of Female Political Ideology: The Cases of Chile and Argentina" was presented at a Women and International Development seminar in the Spring of 1986, and was published as a working paper.

"Alaide Foppa: She Will Not Be Forgotten" was previously published in *Tiger Lily*, Volume 1, Issue 2, 1987.

"A Challenge to Silence: Latin American Women Write" was published in *Women of Power*, Issue 7, Summer 1987.

"Women Artists in Chile: The Conscience of a Country in Crisis" to appear in *Zone*, Spring 1988.

CONTENTS

Dedication

I dedicate these memories of smoke to all of them, as well as to my son, José Daniel, who began to breathe on this earth a short time ago. The book was completed while he was preparing to be born and his arrival is more than a celebration, it is an affirmation that life can still be beautiful and full among so many deaths and torture.

I must especially thank my translator, Janice Malloy, who searched for sounds and words in the English language with care and dedication, and reconstructed these memories so that other audiences would understand what it is to be a Chilean woman in exile in a foreign land. Words of thanks for Ann Wallace, more than an editor, a wise friend who has stimulated me to continue divulging the stories of other countries and the songs of other women. I thank her for her continual encouragement in this very difficult work of being a woman of letters.

It is not easy to live with someone obsessed by words. John Wiggins has shared all of the dreams of my writings, while I recreated these landscapes.

On finishing this manuscript, Delfina Nahuenhual arrived to continue showing me the signs and gestures of love as well as to revere cilantro and search for it desperately in the neat markets of Boston. These memories of smoke are filled with her legacy and her secrets — secrets of a word gestured in silence and a new language, the language of smoke that announces the arrival of the better times through solidarity.

Introduction

My country seems like a child's dream, spongy, aromatic and, at times, grieving before a window of horrors. Dream and vigil, vigil and visions behind the smoke ... I think and I begin to come unstrung when I evoke my special places lost behind the cordillera, encrusted in the snow-covered mountain peaks and submerged in the union of the waters.

I was born in those lands, protected by the self-sacrificing and generous arms of a community of women who, with the patience of the wise, passed its experiences and advice to my mother, who passed them along to me. A balsamic tranquillity embraced us in the remote homes where we innocently followed the route of the birds and invented an atavistic destiny among the rocks.

During my childhood I learned to name, to say, to imagine and, most of all, to invent games and caresses. I was taught to integrate myself completely into our environment because it was *ours*. I savoured the recollection of certain smells: crushed eucalyptus leaves, my grandmother's fragrant tea and the roaring sea that played with the edges of my skirt.

I calmly grew up, saturated more by poetry than by water, because the art of invented words dominated us. From a young age, we knew how to construct metaphors without knowing what we were doing. Nevertheless, a reality of strong dichotomies began to affect my daily existence. I had a collection of beautiful dolls brought from foreign lands, but the neighbours at our beach-house played with pieces of junk and dolls of ragged wool that seemed to carry disease and hunger.

The dogs that approached our house were as ravenous as their owners and shared our dwellings of insanity and neglect. The cold and a humidity filled with sleepiness and foul-smelling fumes complicated their lives and delighted them with the possibilities of death.

So we grew up as "good girls" whipped by the inescapable dichotomies: houses on the beach, winters in the snow, and surrounded by a defeated class of children who tried to approach us cautiously, not to take away our beloved possessions but to imagine the possibility of a life like ours. I would look at the barefoot children, infected and submissive, and at myself in silk stockings. These injustices filled my heart with the question, "Why?"

If I had a motto or political conviction, it did not flourish in the vestibules of my house where perfumed maids brought us dishes of ice-cream and glasses of white wine on silver platters. My convictions grew from something more profound, more powerful: the wounds of the small children who begged near our homes. I use the word, *wounds*, to recall all the wounds of the dispossessed: poorly-treated wounds that begin small and insignificant, scars that slowly become filled with insects and flies that eat the victims to the bone, to the spirit.

I come from an imprisoned and unjust country. We have difficulty looking at ourselves, because the smells of war and rain mix with the memory of the dead. Increasingly, the cordillera imprisoned me, smothered me, my beloved Pacific Ocean crucifying me alive. The children with wounds disturbed my dreams. I began to write, to use writing as an arm to defend, to feel closer to the beloved Chile of my past, to reveal a country trapped behind a veil of smoke.

M.A.

A Challenge to Silence: Latin American Women Write

Censorship has various masks and forms. It may be imposed indirectly by the ruling power, or may be self-imposed by the writer in anticipation of reaction. In the latter case, clandestine publications may become the vehicle for expression, or the writer may seek to veil her message under elaborate metaphors understandable only to an elite few who communicate with each other through such "double-talk." In either case, the effect is the same: to limit one's readers and thus, severely restrict the impact of one's message.

To write as a woman under the gag of authoritarian governments is a double challenge — a challenge to the silence imposed by the fury of the ruling power, and to the denial of a woman's identity as loyal daughter of the homeland. The woman who writes under such circumstances is a "muzzled mouth," for her access to speech, though not denied, is severely restricted. In general, dictatorships instill in a woman a feeling of belonging; they welcome her as a reproducer of the great human specie. Nevertheless, the woman who creates words and not just children does so in defiance of such governments.

The difficulty in being a woman writer in Latin America, as in any country censored by men, lies in the effort to speak through the muzzle imposed by those in power. In several conversations in Vermont between 1979 and 1980, Marta Traba told me that only from exile did she contemplate her country and write about a forbidden theme: the disappeared. Elvira Orphee recalls that her novel, *The Angel's Last Conquest*, is scarcely known in her native country, Argentina, and that only with the overthrow of the dictatorship has it been published there.

Censorship attacks not only the woman who writes but also the woman who reads. Friends have told me that, during the years of repression in Argentina, carrying a book under one's arm was a mark of subversion. Also, the imposition by the government of which books we can or cannot read makes us muzzled beings, prisoners of decrees based on the values of caution, repression and torture.

The two novels analyzed in these pages were written by women who defy censorship by refusing to succumb to silence, women who dare to speak through their anger and intense pain. They risk their lives speaking out for those who have no voice. The Guatemalan Alaide Foppa disappeared in 1980; not a trace of her has been found. Cristina Peri Rossi, an Uruguayan, had to abandon her country for daring to predict the advent of the military government. There are many stories of women who have suffered such a fate. Fortunately, their words remain — words thrown against walls, across continents and against the ears of those who do not want to listen. Beautiful words, words that caress and comfort. Sharp words, words that cut through the muzzle, ungagging the muted. Words like keys, secret codes that seek to open the doors of silenced cities and countries. This is the legacy of the woman who writes in Latin America.

Throughout history, sewing, weaving, knitting and embroidery have been considered to be the feminine legacy. Chatter, gossip and trivial speech from the ultimate stereotype of female discourse. To these assertions, instilled and encrusted in ancient tradition, one must add another category concerning the writings of women, which have traditionally been disdained by literary scholars.

According to Rosario Castellanos, the Latin American woman writer picks up the pen in order to contemplate herself in the mirror of herself.[1] Pioneering women such as the Chilean María Luisa Bombal discovered themselves through their own writing: "Woman is no more than an extension of nature, of everything cosmic and primordial. My female characters possess long hair because hair is the vine that ties them to nature."[2] Along with Bombal, Teresa de la Parra, Norah Lange and Antonia Palacios represent women who unveiled themselves and their experiences through their works.

These women authors were ignored by patronizing editors, vain male writers and hostile literary critics until the 1980s to such a degree that it seemed that women did not write and that those who attempted to do so did it from loneliness, neglect or despair. In this decade, the Latin American woman writer has begun to inscribe herself within a concrete tradition, transforming her particular situation and oppression into a broader perspective. Works such as Marta Traba's *Mothers and Shadows*, Diamela Eltit's *Lumpérica*, Elvira Orphée's *The Angel's Last Conquest*, and Isabel Allende's *House of the Spirits* and *Of Love and Shadows* are narratives that transcend the personal situation of the individual woman and take place in a wider socio-political context.[3]

These works parallel the actual experiences of the female resistance movements such as the Mothers of the Plaza de Mayo in Argentina, the arpillera makers in Chile, and the Mutual Support Group in Guatemala. Like the activist, the Latin American woman writer renounces her status within a sexist society that exiles her from official power, and the ultimate extreme of that chauvinism: brutal, authoritarian dictatorship. The texts written by these women inquire as to the whereabouts of the missing and the tortured. They expose the bitter reality of women raped during torture sessions. In their writings, they address the triple issues of sex, patriarchy and the militaristic society that engenders violence. In this essay, we will examine the ways in which the woman writer denounces the conditions within her society.

Elvira Orphée, born in Argentina in 1930, is one of the first Latin American authors to write from the point of view of a torturer. This is the subject of *The Angel's Last Conquest*, a book that was originally banned in Argentina. It was published in Venezuela, and was only recently allowed in its country of origin. The English translation was published in New York in 1985 by Bantam. Available Press.

The Angel's Last Stand exercises a strong, hypnotic power over the reader, as the author fades into the background and her

characters begin to speak for themselves. The characters speak
of torture using highly technological terms with a frightening and
sinister precision. The banality of evil and its widespread infusion
into society frighten the reader, as one is made aware that torture
techniques can be used in varying degrees for different purposes.
The novel leaves the reader without a doubt that torture is the
dominant act in achieving the ultimate goal: maintaining order
in the state at any cost.

Told by a torturer, the story captures his sense of nostalgia,
of the mission that must be carried out, and of duty to the
homeland. In the chapter entitled "Ceremony," the narrator
passes through his own process of initiation. An ordered and
perfect ritual is performed in the ceremony of torture: "Each
step must be followed, each rule obeyed, each gesture known in
advance" (page 92). In contrast, the victim's role is one of silence.

The relationship of the narrator to Winkel, one of his
superiors in the torture centre, unifies the structure of the
narrative. Winkel is the omnipotent and omnipresent master who
is idealized by his apprentices. The novel progresses from the
narrator's initiation, in which a certain identification between
victim and torturer is produced, until the moment when the
narrator occupies the same position as Winkel. The torturer sinks
into a world of an ordered and precise insanity, making his escape
impossible.

A clear theme of the novel is the treatment of the female
political prisoner, who is abused at two levels: as a prisoner and
as a woman. Sexual violation is used again and again as a method
of obtaining information and breaking her spirit for the sake of
political gain. The narrator makes the following observation
concerning a woman prisoner brought to the torture centre:

> *One day they brought a woman who must have
> been arrested with immense brutality, to judge by
> her appearance. It wouldn't have been a good idea
> to detain her in an accessible facility because the
> family lawyers would have tracked her down. Three*

of them fucked her. She was pretty. I didn't feel like touching her, not because I was a newlywed as they said, and not because I didn't feel like mixing business with pleasure, but because the relationship between the bodies we touch and our own should be different (page 91).

The constant allusions to the woman's body as the property of the state and of the torturer is one of the jolting aspects of *The Angel's Last Conquest*, because it is through this recognition that we are distanced from the torturer whom we have come to know as an adolescent initiated in the ceremonies of insanity and fear. Each victim that he possesses is another advance in his prolific career, and only the reader's questions remain: How can this torturer live in the same city? How can he have a family? How can he return home after work? Can he possibly love and care for others? These questions float and remain unanswered for the perplexed reader who must attempt to reconcile these two worlds: the human world of love and caring, and the world of dictatorships, characterized by torture, rape and death.

Marta Traba's *Mothers and Shadows*, published in English in 1985 by Readers International, takes place in the spaces occupied by victims who roam through the cities, travelling like phantoms in countries populated by memories of the missing. Those who survive must live among the torturers and the tortured. *Mothers and Shadows* is a dialogue between two women of different generations sharing memories of what the political repression in three countries of the Southern Cone has cost them. One recalls her lost son, missing in some part of Chile since the beginning of the military coup in 1973. The other remembers her period of political activism in Buenos Aires, her subsequent imprisonment and the loss of her child while she was in jail. *Mothers and Shadows* sums up the feelings of these silent victims, humiliated in the torture chambers for having committed the crime of being different or of having the name of someone "subversive" in their address books.

Each woman has chosen a different path: one suffered imprisonment while the other chose retreat and absence. The nausea of surviving the hell of torture is contrasted with the nausea of living in a place where so many have disappeared. Each of the women has suffered from the grief caused by the disappearance of a loved one, by the fact that there is no body to bury, only the aching void of an unexplained absence. One character says: "For a moment, I convinced myself that hell was better than limbo. Anything better than limbo." The other woman adds: The worst part of coming back to Montevideo is to ask about people who surely are dead, have been tortured or have disappeared" (page 30).

The novel's power lies in its revelation of the total usurpation of one's personal life by the dictatorship. In an atmosphere of asphyxia and terror where the individual exists or does not exist according to the whim of the state, the ultimate question becomes: How to survive the menace one more day? The fascination and wonder in the world is constricted, cut off for those under dictatorship, those who must live every day facing menace, pain and, too often, death.

The protagonists of *Mothers and Shadows* are linked by their solitude, their common suffering, and the intense desire to communicate in an empty country inhabited by the ghosts of the disappeared. They share a world of terror and a desire to create; they are not satisfied to be mere witnesses of a passing world. "Ah," says one, "The brief time we spent together isn't important. The intensity is what counts. The world we glimpsed, the fear we shared. And I don't mind telling you that my hands are perpetually frozen and that they'd gladly, gladly reach out to you for warmth. Let's take things one at a time, sister; let's see if we create or are merely witnesses" (page 102). Herein lies an essential characteristic of the writing of Latin American women: they take up the pen not merely to observe, but to vindicate the silence and to act, to use the power of the word to denounce the plight of their people and their countries.

This denunciation occurs in the two texts studied above from different perspectives, reflected in the narrators' point of view. The narrator of *The Angel's Last Conquest* elaborates the masculine ceremonies of a patriarchal world that involve the pain and humiliation of the victims. In defiance of this world, the narrators of *Mothers and Daughters* create a universe of female voices absorbed in the process of healing and finding a sense of sisterhood amidst the death and destruction. Both novels have as their central theme the victimizing nature of a system that enslaves the torturer as well as the tortured.

The Angel's Last Conquest and *Mothers and Daughters* represent two instances of the same coordinate. Each novel reveals the infrastructure of societies that use torture as a means of control. They expose the repression taking place under Latin American dictatorships by breaking the silence of their victims. By telling their stories, these writers themselves create the possibility of life and hope amidst the horror, evil and cruelty.

FOOTNOTES

1 Rosario Castellanos has been one of the Latin American women writers who has contributed toward a school of thought on and a theoretical definition of women's writing. These ideas originate from *Women Who Know Latin* (Mexico: Septentas, 1973).

2 From an interview with Lucia Guerra in *The Narrative of María Luisa Bombal: A Vision of the Feminine Existence* (Madrid: Playor, 1984, p. 67). María Luisa Bombal was one of the most innovative Latin American women writers of the 1940s. Her most famous work in English is *The Final Mist* (New York: Farrar and Strauss, 1984).

3 The two books analyzed in this study are *Conversación al Sur* (Buenos Aires, Argentina: Siglo XXI) and its English translation, *Mothers and Shadows* (London: Readers International, 1985); and *La última tortura del Angel* (Venezuela: Monteavila, 1977), in English, *The Angel's Last Conquest* (New York: B. Available Press, 1985).

4 For general information on the bibliographies of Traba and Orphee see Evelyn Picon Garfield, *Women's Voices from Latin America* (Detroit: Wayne State University Press, 1985).

Landscapes

This winter landscape, suspended in silence and covered by a cloak of silken snow, reminds me of the strangeness of those unforgettable distances we call *exiles*.

The snow reminds me that I am getting further and further away from Chile, from my country's smells, closer to sun than to ice. This spectacular snow, newly fallen on the immense, silent streets, is a witness to the fact that I am a foreigner. Always I notice that there are no Andean mountains here, or rivers into which the freshly-melted waters from the mountains flow.

I am in a snowing city, and I celebrate the premature transparency, the whiteness. I know that I am growing more and more distant from my cities, my ports that smell of smoke, and my oceans smelling of water, not ice.

Landscapes dismember and fragment, make us realize that we are inhabitants of borrowed territories. I am frightened as I watch the neighbourhood children approach to celebrate the falling of the first flakes. Memory transports me to a past, where I see other children, children who speak my language, who laugh at my words. I see them leaving happily with parents to go to the mountains close to Santiago to see the first snowfall in ten years in the capital city.

I close my eyes, and this whiteness fills me with despair, its silent odour provoking me. A whiteness that reminds me, that says, *you are far from the sun of Latin America, you are far from the grapes of the Elqui Valley, you are far from your Delfina.*

The landscape of my country is chaotic and disorganized. In the southern regions, there are enormous blizzards of snow and wind. Small boats, enchanting and skillful, unfurl their sails through channels of the devil, of life itself. The world's southern-most city, Punto Arenas, a city of snow, but because of its distance, is foreign to the inhabitants of the central zones, where the landscape is marked by a chain of fertile and tranquil mountains called the Coastal Mountains, as well as the impetuous and feared Andes.

We live within these geographic monstrosities — alienated, massacred and sleepy. Nevertheless, these are my territories, my trees, my trash, my pains next to the barefoot or the clothed. The landscape of my country infiltrated by eyes that are learning to look and not see, to distort and, yet want.

In New England where I now live, the snow is beautiful — a silence suspended between footprints. Everything explodes in this silence. Everything explodes within my words, alienating the elegant, methodical rhythms of the snow, far from my loves and close to the window.

I imagine the snow becomes water, the water becomes rocks, the rocks become sand. I imagine that I am near the sand and the sea of my childhood. I hear my mother's precise footsteps and I imagine all of the happiness and security of the world in this scene.

I close my eyes, the fierce and intermittent sun of this white litany before me, and I see my mother with her pockets full of seaweed, small shells and stones. She glows in the light, washed by the ocean wind. She offers me these gifts calmly and says, *"Here is the universe."* Within this strange window I turn, and in this foreign house, my hand in my pockets finds stones, shells, and sun, water of my country.

I am happy. The snow looks like the sea, and the sea, the Andean Mountains. I weave, I discover. I name my landscapes.

The Blue Teacups

November in Stockholm. A light and delicate darkness slowly surrounds the city as if, little by little, the wide and angular sky was beginning to prepare for the great polar night, a night of an immense, greenish sun. The lights of the city begin to wither with the grace of an agile ballerina. In a twilight full of veils and nostalgia, it is as though the candles of generous spirits surround the city, giving off a light that invites the peace that can only be achieved through silence and the night.

I become part of this magic and rare luminosity. I walk through alleys that seem to be populated by the goblins of Nordic legend, so alien and yet so familiar, because it is difficult to feel like a stranger among all the blonde heads. At times, I walk hurriedly; other times, I slow down to contemplate a thin hand as it reaches out to light a candle in a bare window.

A small candle at the end of the street calls my attention, and I am overcome by a need to climb the stairs of the illuminated house, to pound on the door as if beckoned by a distant voice. Nevertheless, I must remember that I am far from my Latin America where, despite the disappearances, pains and daily kicks in the stomach, we still dare to enter a neighbour's house with the sole purpose of passing time.

The candle seems to mark the route of my pilgrimage; its undulating fragrance pleases me in this darkness of goblins. I begin to ascend the staircase that calls to me. I do not know if I am naive, astute, or sleepwalking as I respond to the call.

I discover that I have arrived at a wake. There are no bodies, only belongings. The women who are spectators at births and funerals silently hang old tapestries on the bare walls. They hide the broken shoes of the dead woman and, as if enchanted, they clean some blues teacups with golden edges. They are the most beautiful teacups I have ever seen. I ask myself if they belonged to an elderly woman presiding like a queen over a family drawing room. Or if they belonged to a forgotten spinster caring for the vestiges of her family and her own loneliness.

I stop to contemplate the cups; they are as blue as the ocean or my grandmother's eyes. They remind me of bodies that shine with desire, after making love. They smell of travel and elegance, and surely belonged on a table of golden wood. Perhaps they were bought at a pawnshop at the end of the war.

I do not know whether I should ask about the history of the blue teacups or to try to learn from the enigmas of that which is left unsaid. I discover that the cups belonged to a Jewish woman from Hungary, and that they are from distant Bohemia. The woman never let go of her teacups. In times of leisure and happiness, she contemplated them.

These teacups hold the stories of many exiles. They have travelled, have been buried in earthquakes, and have survived the loss of children and homes. I cannot stop looking at them. I find my eyes full of the roads of my great-grandmother Elena. The one who had to leave her house, her feather pillows, her histories and her memories one morning because she was Jewish. She carried her bronze padlocks across the Atlantic and the Pacific Oceans until she arrived in the port of Valparaiso in Chile, where she planted flowers and found a new place to hang her keys.

Now I bring the blue teacups from Stockholm to Boston. They seem like the veins of lost children that search for the familiarity of smiling faces or a piece of bread on a friendly table. The teacups are in my home. I care for them and love them because I preserve the water of so many exiles in them. The exile of the woman from Bohemia who, before dying, must have left me the message to care for her most precious memories. I also imagine them in the home of my grandmother in Vienna, full of fragrances and bits of orange.

I will never know the true history of the blue teacups. Perhaps someone will come to look for them and will return them to their true home. Until them, I will look at them, celebrate and love them.

Rivers

Rivers, chromatic and beautiful, have an uneven texture. Fragments of rejuvenated life, also instances of unannounced death.

My country's rivers resemble leafy and generous trees intuitively suspended between earth and sky. We have mountain rivers, small belts of water that sparkle, narrow passages that allow only a small trickle of clear water to descend from the majestic and overwhelming cordillera.

Gabriela Mistral spoke of rivers because rivers spoke to her. I imagine her barefoot, her hands open, collecting water, *blessed water* from the mountain, water of our America.

There are other wild and feverish rivers that plough through the possessions of those ephemeral inhabitants who naively construct cardboard dwellings on the banks of a treacherous river. The river, a familiar tyrant, robs children of their defenseless ragdolls and drags away their skeletal cows, the only sustenance for the large families of those distant regions.

But there are gentle rivers full of small, blue bubbles where women meet to wash their clothes. Standing or kneeling on firm rocks, illuminated by the sun and the simple happiness of the dispossessed, they begin the ceremonies of laundry at dawn.

They dry their rags in the sun, tell tales, laugh and, at times, moan over hunger or perhaps their husband's desertion. The gentle river shelters them, listens to them. The image of white clothes in baskets of bubbles makes them feel good again. They sing, softly and warmly and the river responds to their voices with a sweet and shifting litany. Bubbles float in the air and perch on the heads of the washerwomen.

In my country, I have also seen *other* rivers, not the devouring wild rivers, not the ones that march to the beat of certain songs. They are rivers of men who rob scraps of human life. They are rivers of cadavers dispassionately thrown from helicopters of death. They are rivers where detached heads, mutilated intestines, eyes and ears habitually float.

In my country, I have seen rivers — signs of death. I have approached them to recognize bodies, to cover them with the linen of white peace. How does one recognize a battered body? Fix a broken arm? The rivers of Chile ache, like the rivers of Argentina. Women kneel by the banks of the river at dawn. They gather the dead, covered by the waters of greed, and dig graves next to the river of insomnia, cover bodies with soil and flowers.

The rivers of my country wound me. I would love to return to them — find them clean with the smell of life and fresh moss. I would cover myself with the porous water, kiss the one I love. I would become one with all the rivers of my country.

The Wanderers

Three faces float in my memory: my celestial grandmother with her fish-like gaze, my mother, distant and crazy with a forgetful nostalgia, and my nanny, my Delfina, the magician who cared for us, bathed us with the sweet balsam of her skin. I recreate them now in this landscape so alien from my own. Where mornings are painful as sharpened knives and the sun is not so generous as the dignified and disturbed light of my country, of Latin America.

My three mothers would sit in the well-groomed garden of my grandmother's elegant house, gently fanning themselves in litany. They would talk about their pains, their fears and more than anything, about their own cobwebbed memories.

My grandmother would incessantly recount how she crossed the Andes on a mule. How her family was well-travelled but eccentric when they arrived in Buenos Aires from distant Russia. How they later established themselves in that narrow and delicious longitude called Chile. My grandmother travelled by mule with my great-grandmother, Sonia, mother of seven children and former seamstress to a czarina. Now a poor, Jewish immigrant with a few words of Spanish, her voice cracking with all the hope of the dispossessed.

It was in this way they arrived in Chile, crossing the slopes, penetrating the soft and stormy landscapes of the Andes until they settled in the city of Osorno, the land of German colonists and, most possibly, the Nazis. It was the sweet, summertime eyes of my grandfather, José, and the celestial look of my grandmother, Josefina, who managed to eradicate the hatred of so many wars and attract other Jews marked by the claws of concentration camps.

In Osorno, my grandparents bought land, cooked in large country ovens, loved and loved life. They made great friends, like the Saez family who owned a funeral parlour where my mother played as a child among the coffins. Perhaps for these reasons, she loves life so much, does not fear death.

My grandparent's faces, from so many voyages, acquired the forms and waves of wanderers. In Osorno, so close to the earth, they learned to bake bread in huge, clay ovens. My mother remembers the small, bare feet of the country children that always shocked her. She would play among the coffins, and, in the frosty evenings, she would hide in them to shelter herself from the rain.

After a brief stay in the South, my travelling grandmother followed her wandering Sonia, to Mamiña, located on the outskirts of Iquique. My grandfather became a travelling salesman while living in this saltpeter town.

My grandmother Josefina recounts how in Mamiña, the wild air of the desert, the Camanchaca, constantly covered them with dust like an omen of funereal calamity. When the Camanchaca arrived, the women would take refuge in their enormous houses with only the damned sand boring into their flesh. Josefina's oldest daughter died in the Camanchaca. They buried her in that desolate hamlet in a small, white coffin, recalling the salt and pain of dead children.

From the desert, the family moved to Santiago, the capital city where I grew up and learned to always feel protected by the enormous white wings of the Andes.

In Santiago, my mother, grandmother and nanny lived together. Of course, I had my father, my grandfathers and brothers, but it was always the women who braided my hair and told me stories. My grandmother continually knitted enormous, multi-colored scarves. If I could choose a way to die, I would suffocate in my grandmother's spongy scarves.

My nanny, Delfina, an involuntary wanderer, always seemed to sit in a spot behind my mother and grandmother. Born in Chillán, the heart of the pottery region, Delfina's face was molded from a sad, dark clay, the so-called Quinchamali clay. She served us our food in the back rooms but to me, she was never a servant but instead a magical sorcerer who lived on the border of a borrowed kingdom. An immense earthquake around 1920 forced this woman of earth to abandon Chillán and left her without a house, a husband or children.

Delfina Nahuenhual, wearing a shawl and self-confidence, boarded a third-class train to the capital city. Somehow, she ended up at my grandparents' house, remained there for almost forty years, learned Viennese cooking and my grandmother's customs, continuing to tell us unbelievable stories from the South.

My mother had to leave the country for many relentless and complicated reasons. At times, she says it was for political reasons. When she spoke of politics, I used to think she was referring to an aunt or an illness, but I soon learned that politics meant everything. Suddenly we became strangers in our country where the right to speak had become a public danger, and we packed our bags. I said goodbye to all of my dead — especially my grandfather José who loved Chile so much and was himself loved by so many. I always believed that, in his green eyes, I carried the ferns and the forests, the summer of my country.

We kissed my confused grandmother who knitted an immense white scarf faster than ever.

• • •

And so, by fate, I became and am a wanderer. I, too, have just given birth to a child. I, too, will have to invent a country for him. Tell him about Delfina Nahuenhual, those dawns and a hearth full of goblins and stories. Tell him how Delfina smelled of smoke and oregano. Tell him that his grandmother played among the coffins because she was, and still is, in love with life. I will tell him about nights in front of a low fire and journeys spent looking at stars, the Southern Cross, that clear, shy, milky path.

And if my child asks me where I am from, I will tell him that I carry a country within myself. Like all women, I carry my home in my hair and carry love in my body full of spirits and pilgrimages.

Communities

I am often asked if I have developed a community of friends, acquaintances and contacts in the small, suburban town where I live. For me, there is incongruity in this question, because a community is not something that is planned or searched for — it emerges spontaneously. I often think about daily life in my country and in other Latin American countries, an America as homogeneous in its instability as in its generosity.

In Latin America, the community exists in the streets. It exists in the daily contact among commuters waiting for a bus, in the animated conversation between a street seller and a customer. Community can be found in a conversation that begins in a café and ends over a glass of wine in a bar. It exists in the compassion, the pity and the immense affection one feels for a beggar with injured hands, or for a young person who has just been beaten. When we go out into the streets in Latin America, we are met and battered by the voices of castoffs, fugitives and individuals who have been mutilated, body and soul. This spectrum of humanity forms a community profiled in zones of happiness and pain.

Here in North America, communities are constructed by neighbourhood, the colour of one's skin, by children or sexual preference. Sharp and rigid classifications. In the United States, it is strange and seldom one sees a beautiful, round grandmother arm-in-arm with her twenty-year old granddaughter. For me, this is a common and visual reflection of a community in my America.

Community networks in the United States form microcosms of the city in which they exist. For example, women organize friendships according to their husband's clubs and their children's schools. They form bonds of familiar contact at their churches. When life fails and disintegrates, the North American does not know where to turn, to seek help and support and so, in solitude and terror, searches for answers in thousands of books that begin with, "How to ..."

In Latin America, the family is integrated, people of diverse ages, friends of the parents who become friends of the children. This structure provides a certain equilibrium and enrichment, a sense of community that is not imposed but one that is born spontaneously. People are more free to make mistakes, touch each other and greet each other daily with hugs and kisses. The Spanish are wise to kiss on the cheek, not once but twice.

Communities in Latin America are full of women who possess magical knowledge. There are communities of matrons who give advice during childbirth and wakes. There are communities of nannies who rock us to sleep, feed us and enclose us in a universe full of mirrors and explanations for the inexplicable.

There are communities of daily scenes: markets where we contemplate multi-coloured pills, braids of garlic and nets full of fish. There are communities of beauty parlours where we learn the delicious intrigues of our neighbours. While beauticians fuss with our hair, we find out about neighbourhood love affairs, the horrors of the people in the house on the corner, who has been arrested. The fact that the community talks and gossips is healthy and indicates an interest in others, regardless of how far removed they are from one's own circumstances.

Here, Anglo-Saxons choose caution, silence, thousands of masks that deny pain, anger, and forgetfulness. In North American hair salons, there is a strong odour of cleanliness, symmetry of well-groomed hair.

It is obvious that Latin Americans are different and diverse — we have different histories and landscapes. Despite our poverty and inability to pay our international debts, despite our insufficient medical system, we have discovered another type of development — the development of a spirit that trusts others and, is more vulnerable, a spirit more open to hugs, to clandestine encounters, to daily insecurities and to life.

When asked if I have a community in Wellesley, Massachusetts, I would have to say yes, it is my friends, those who speak my language, and no one else. The block I live on is a horizon of mute houses. The suburbs are dull. My community is located in the streets of my childhood, in doorsteps full of old women and birds. That is where I am constantly drawn, for inside myself, I have never left home.

The House on the Corner

My grandparents lived on a quiet, neighbourhood street corner where the light hemmed the cloudless sky, bare to the immense branches of a palm tree located in the centre of the garden like a faithful and familiar guardian. We were happy in the house on the corner while life passed in the gentle community of Nuñoa, former neighbourhood of the lesser aristocracy, now changed by the arrival of an infernal meat market that used to infuriate my father and me. I would tremble with fear when I saw huge Don Giovanni parade with his knife tainted by fresh blood, knowingly tormenting the neighbourhood children.

My grandparent's house contained doors and windows. It was easy to hide in the small closets similar to enchanted cellars where heads of garlic and eucalyptus leaves were stored to improve one's health and attract good spirits. Our relationship with the neighbours was polite. I was friends with Luchito, the son of señora Monica, owner of the small store on the corner. We spent a lot of time playing in dark and light rooms. Many, many years later, I found out that Luchito had committed suicide.

We used to spend every Sunday with my grandfather walking around the block. Stunned by the scent of peaches or the splendid illumination of the Andes, we would stumble on every rock and dog in the road. And we were happy. On his arm, I felt like a small princess escorted by an elegant gentleman. We often passed by Irma Miller's house, and admired the peace of her well-groomed garden and the leaves piled up in rays of autumn light. At the time, we did not know who lived in that house; I only discovered her identity ten years later.

One day, my father told us we had to leave the country. No one wanted to cry, but each of us carried a small handful of soil in our pockets, and my sister brought a bottle of water from the beach where she met her first love.

In a foreign land, our pain and nostalgia were accentuated, our memories eventually converted into a strange lethargy. When I grew older, I returned to my country and to the house on the corner. I went again with my grandfather to contemplate the victorious domes of the Andes and the flowering peach trees. But so many things had changed — the censorship, the silence, the curfew, but more than anything, Irma's house.

On one of those trips of returns and good-byes, I learned, intuitively, of my grandfather's death. I imagined him dreaming and burying himself deeper and deeper in the immense palm tree by the house. I knew he was happy and I celebrated his death which, for me, has been a little piece of life enlightening me in my exile.

More than ten years have passed since my grandfather's death. The government has burned many people during those years, young people, parents and their children. They have burned the works of writers, have robbed Irma of a son.

It is not worthwhile to analyze the details of how I met Irma, only that, when I went to see her, I remembered the little pillows of leaves next to her door. It was then that I first cried over my grandfather's death. Irma Miller was the owner of a lovely house. She cared for her family, including her two sons and a grand-daughter, and made sure that the streets were swept in the fall. She baked bread to give to the old women in the neighbourhood and, during the warm Santiago afternoons, she would sit, happy to be able to waste time and feel close to her son, Juan.

Juan disappeared in 1975, two years after the military coup. He was a young cinematographer with a brilliant future, like so many others. Irma has never been able to bury her son because she does not know where he is and, after thirteen ominous years, she no longer knows who to ask if he is dead or alive, or why he was killed, or what jail he is in.

We always end up talking about Juan. She has taught me to see him everywhere, because he is everywhere, especially in Irma's soft, trembling hands while she creates arpilleras — hard, simple and deep, like her pain. Arpilleras are beautiful, embroidered tapestries made by the relatives of missing people to raise money for their long quest for information concerning the fate of their loved ones. Trees, branches, a radiant sun and a young woman with a baby in her arms all sprang from Irma's hands.

What are Irma's nights like? She must ask herself where they took Juan, where they left his badly injured body, where to look for him. But the only response she receives is silence, the terrifying silence of complicity.

Irma Miller and my grandfather, Irma Miller and all of us, so many different destinies marked by a fate replete with tyrants and torturers. The executioner, the one who blindfolded Juan Miller for a second and forever, is in each café and on every corner. Despite the gags and bonds, Juan always visits his mother. He kisses her while she contemplates the passing of time or while she recounts her grandchildren's pranks.

My grandfather José and the house on the corner have remained like scraps of memory, the sun illuminating new paths. Now, only Irma's face is left, saying goodbye, asking me not to forget her. In the distance, I hear the familiar sounds of Don Giovanni's knives. Someone takes me by the arm, and I turn as if in a whirlwind of stars.

Without realizing it, I return to the corner. It is still light, and the large, fat and generous palm tree stretches out. Maybe Grandpa José awaits us wearing the hat from his beloved Vienna, maybe Juan has reappeared, marked by suns. Maybe we are all returning.

A Visit to the Mothers of the Plaza de Mayo

Sunday in the Plaza de Mayo. August. It is almost the end of winter in South America, and the first buds are starting to swell, a sign of the spring we have all been waiting for, one that might bring an answer to one of the most overwhelming and emotional questions of the Argentinean people: the fate of those who disappeared during the evil years of the dirty war, la guerra sucia.[1]

A limpid sun lights up the Plaza de Mayo this Sunday. Young fathers and their children are feeding the pigeons. Everything looks prosperous. The women of the capital are wearing elegant leather suits this season; the children are well-dressed. All these signs of well-being give the eerie sensation that nothing unusual has happened in this plaza. The appearance of normality is deceiving, for this spot where I sit, caressed by the benign sun of early spring, is the same place that has become a major symbol of protest, witness, and denunciation of the crimes committed by the military Juntas of Argentina.

To make a brief recapitulation of recent historical events, the armed forces of Argentina took power on March 16, 1976. They dissolved all political parties; labour unions and all universities were put under government control. Public statements of the Junta declared these measures were taken "to restore order and peace to the country". Similar measures were taken in Chile in 1973 by the Pinochet dictatorship. In both countries, in addition to the official, announced measures, another level of measures was instituted: a subterranean rule began to take shape that used undeclared and unavowed methods of terror, repression, suspicion, torture, disappearance and murder to put down opposition. At first, the victims were known opponents, such as labour union members, university activists, or journalists. Later, the choice of victims was what one can only describe as random.

Translated by Cola Franzen and Janice Molloy

As the crimes increased, so did the need to keep the subterranean war hidden, and the attempts to hide all traces of the horrendous actions became more outrageous. The military embarked on a kind of final solution with their policy of "disappearing" citizens in greater and greater numbers.

As unbelievable as it may seem to us now, what began as a clandestine operation became, with time, routine and bureaucratic. The squads of terror settled down to using teams of men dressed in civilian clothes and driving black Falcons without license plates, who entered homes or places of work at will, in broad daylight or at night, to seize and drag off people who for one reason or another were thought to be suspicious, or who were just unlucky enough to be in that place at that time. Sometimes totally innocent individuals were taken, including children and even babies. Most of those seized went on to endure clandestine prisons, torture, disappearance and, in many cases, death. The open kidnappings sowed an atmosphere of fear and terror throughout the entire population.

Now the country is left to relive this painful era, to uncover what was so assiduously covered up. Where are those who disappeared without trace? What happened to the children snatched along with their parents? What happened to the babies that women carried in their arms as they went to prison? What became of the babies born to imprisoned women? We have begun to know answers to some of these questions, but not to all of them, and justice requires an answer to all questions. Mothers, grandmothers and wives of the disappeared have been forced by tragic necessity to rescue their lost ones from the oblivion intended by the Juntas, to inquire into the destiny of the estimated 9,000 people who disappeared between 1973 and the return to democracy in 1984.

The years from 1973 to 1975, saw many disappearances as well as a series of disruptive activities carried out by urban guerrillas. The actions of both sides created such a climate of mistrust and tension in the country that, for some time, people did not know who was responsible for the kidnappings and killings. Later, it became known that paramilitary groups of the extreme right, operating under the clear protection of the military of the democratically elected Perons, were responsible for the disappearances. It was not the urban guerrillas as the military tried to pretend.[2]

The political situation in Argentina has always been an anomaly; it is a prosperous country with many natural resources, yet has always been politically unstable. To recapitulate briefly and to shed some light on this situation, in 1930, the Argentinean armed forces overthrew the democratically elected government of Hipólito Irigoyen of the Radical Civic Union Party. Since then, the military has overthrown five other legally elected governments, and has ruled Argentina for a longer period than all of the democratic governments together.

Juan Perón was a colonel who participated in the coup d'etat that overthrew President Ramon Carillo. He used his position as the head of the National Labour Department to take control of the developing trade unions, which he corrupted and used as a tool for his own personal gains. Perón became president for the first time in 1946 and was overthrown in 1955. In 1973 Perón, who had by then become a cult figure in Argentina, returned to power. Even though Perón was chosen to be president, there were many fascists in the armed forces, and they were instrumental in the creation of the paramilitary groups even before the coup. After he died in 1974, Isabel, his second wife, became president, but on March 24, 1976 the military took power and the dirty war began. They dismissed the congress and obsessively took on the mission of ridding the country of what they referred to as subversive thought of any kind.[3]

You may be asking yourself, who were these people who disappeared? The answer is anybody at all who might possibly have been perceived as opposing the regime. One did not have to act openly against the dictatorship to be a candidate for a disappearance. One could just think one's own private thoughts and still be found guilty. Statistics show that 30 percent of the disappeared were workers, 21 percent were students, and 10 percent were professionals. The rest included anyone who happened to be caught in the net, including teenagers, housewives, and even babies, as we said earlier.

The world, especially a silenced and silent Argentina, has been shaken to learn, from the testimony of survivors and by subsequent excavations of unmarked graves, that the disappeared were tortured and finally killed. Many were thrown into the Rio de la Plata or into the sea from helicopters. Some of the recovered bodies showed death by drowning, that is, that the people were still alive when they were thrown out. Certain groups were subjected to especially sadistic treatment, for instance women and Jews. For the treatment of Jews in captivity, see Jacobo Timmerman's testimony in *Prisoner Without a Name, Cell Without a Number*. Women were not arrested particularly because they were women, but *because* they were women, they were subjected to rape and other violations in addition to torture in the clandestine prisons. It has been determined that a quarter of the disappeared were women, and of those, 10 percent were pregnant at the time of their arrest.

The state of limbo in which the families of the disappeared found themselves caused them to begin a quest to find their loved ones, even if only their bones.[4] In 1975, the mothers and wives of the disappeared started on a tortuous trek of searching which eventually led them to a period of reflection. When they went to police stations or jails to ask about the whereabouts of their children they were often told: "It's your own fault, Señora, for raising a subversive". Or they would say: "Your son is in the underground and is outside the country".

There are many groups of women in Latin America that have developed in authoritarian regimes. For example, in Chile a group of women formed the Asociación de Detenidos-Desaparecidos (Association of the Detained-Disappeared) in order to find their loved ones. This association was founded in 1975, and carries out a variety of protest activities, including night vigils and political marches. A similar group developed in Guatemala in 1979 called Grupo de Ayuda Mutual (Mutual Aid Group).

This group consisted of about thirty women who carried out activities similar to those of the association in Chile. The groups vary in size; they usually have between 30 and 50 members. These women's groups are almost always formed by mothers, housewives who have been forced to leave their private spheres and go into the streets to find their loved ones.

Because there still exists in Argentine society the legacy of Spanish culture that treats *mothers* with a certain respect and even veneration, these mothers were treated by police and police officials with superficial politeness, but were never given a straight answer to their questions. With the guidance of leaders such as Perez Esquivel, the Argentinean human rights activist who was awarded the Nobel Peace Prize in 1981, the Mothers began to request concrete actions, such as asking for a writ of habeas corpus to be issued in specific cases. They still received no response to their requests.

The women then asked themselves, What could they do? What power did they actually possess? Who might make an impact in the face of such indifference? Who might have the information they sought? The group now known as the Mothers of the Plaza de Mayo was born in 1977 from this examination of the possibilities available to them. In the beginning, it was not a formal organization but simply a group of women who decided to join together to protest. Their protests took place then as now in this same plaza where children are playing and feeding the pigeons.

The Plaza de Mayo was a strategic location for a public demonstration. Here, Argentinean independence was proclaimed in 1810. Here, Juan Perón gave his populist speeches. In fact, the Plaza de Mayo is not only the heart of Buenos Aires, it is the heart of the country. The buildings that surround it include the old Cabildo, the Town Hall; the Presidential Palace called the Casa Rosada ("Pink House") because of its pink stone; and a number of other important government buildings and churches.

In the centre of the plaza, there is an obelisk that celebrates the 400th anniversary of the city's founding. On a cool April day at five o'clock in the afternoon, a few women appear in the plaza and start circling the obelisk. Each one wears a white kerchief on her head with the names of her disappeared ones embroidered around the edge, together with the date of their disappearance. The women march in absolute silence. The demonstrators, the mothers of the Plaza de Mayo, are mainly working and middle-class women, because these groups were most affected by the repression. There are some upper-class women, but they constitute a minority.

This civic and cooperative action on the part of a handful of women without any political power, for the most part traditional housewives who had never taken part in any public action before, was the *only public protest* made for a long time against the traffickers of death in Argentina. They were the *only ones* to stand up in favor of life. In his book, *The Madwomen of the Plaza de Mayo*, Jean Pierre Bousquet expressed the significance of this first demonstration: "When on a Thursday of April of 1977 at five o'clock in the afternoon, fourteen women, between 40 and 70 years of age, defied the ban on public gatherings promulgated by the all-powerful Military Junta and marched in the Plaza de Mayo to make known their pain and their resolve not to accept having their questions go unanswered, the generals lost their first battle."[5]

The demonstrations every Thursday in the plaza are now an event, a tradition and a symbol that the Argentinean people refuse to submit to fascism, but the example was started and carried on for years by a handful of women. In the beginning, soldiers would appear and simply ask them to disperse. However, as time went on and as the demonstrations grew in size and began to have a public impact, the Junta began to make reprisals. In 1978, they kidnapped the group's first leader, Azuzena Villaflor de Vicenti, together with eleven other members of the group. At about the same time, they also kidnapped two French nuns who they later gave the sadistic name of "The Flying Nuns" because they were thrown into the sea from a helicopter after being tortured. Doña Azuzena suffered terrible tortures and martyrdom. The location of her remains is still unknown. The others kidnapped with her were finally released after an international outcry, organized mostly by the United Nations. Regardless of this violent action against nuns, the clergy in Argentina has not been involved in protest as it has been in the case of Chile; on the contrary, the clergy has been so quiet that it has been accused of collaborating with the military. Likewise, liberation theology is not an issue for the Mothers.

At the beginning, very few women gathered; the initial number was, to be exact, thirteen. Then, other women followed, and from 1976 to the present there have usually been between 50 and 60 women marching. The same mothers march, but as the years went by and people stopped being so afraid, there were more and more people joining them. Now, people may not necessarily be mothers, but are sympathetic to the cause. The plaza activity is an outward and physical demonstration of the many things that go on in these people's lives. For example, they have weekly meetings and create new strategies of protest. These strategies vary from seeking public support in other nations to organizing national protest involving other human rights organizations. I believe the mothers have become the heroines of Argentinean society, for people realize that they were the only ones who dared to speak in a silent society. Yet they are in a difficult position with regard to President Alfonsín, because the mothers, as the voice of conscience, want all of the people responsible for the murders to be tried. Alfonsín has said that he will only try those who gave the orders.[6]

What is important to remember is that the Mothers of the Plaza de Mayo have a tremendous historical importance. Even if they did not contribute directly to the fall of the military, they serve as an example to other non-violent groups in Latin America.

It was not until 1979 that the group of women became cohesive enough to organize themselves officially into the Mothers of the Plaza de Mayo. They collected the twenty names necessary to satisfy the legal requirement to form an association at the risk of their lives. They found a location where they could meet and elect their leaders by secret ballot. The leaders have so far been women who are truly fearless, who refuse to be terrorized, and who inspire confidence in others, women such as the present leader, Hebe de Bonafini.

The Mothers began to have an international impact. Some travelled to Europe in 1979 and asked for and were granted an audience with the Pope. However, they really became known world-wide in 1978 when the World Cup Soccer competition was held in Buenos Aires, and the city was filled with journalists from all over the world. The demonstrations in the plaza were photographed and appeared in the newspapers, magazines and on the television screens of the five continents. The Mothers realized then that visibility and publicity were powerful weapons of protest. Though they had no political contacts and no previous experience in political affairs, they showed real shrewdness in planning and continuing their actions. They became more and more effective, in spite of censorship, in spite of silence, in spite of ostracism. Sometimes even members of their own families refused to have anything to do with these women because they were afraid. Many people were afraid to associate with families of the disappeared. It was considered dangerous, and undoubtedly was.

Just as the World Cup brought the cause of the Mothers to the world, a larger public began to be aware of the Argentinean atrocities and the stories of the disappeared through the Argentine movie, *The Official Story*, which tells of a typical middle-class family, unaware of the brutalities. The mother soon begins to suspect that her adopted daughter could be the child of someone who had been kidnapped and murdered. The rest of the movie involves this woman's increasing awareness of the atrocities that took place in her beloved country, and the impact that this knowledge has on her relationship with her husband and child.

The Mothers of the Plaza de Mayo are still visible and extremely active, even after the military was pressured to return to the barracks in 1984. The size of the demonstrations has increased with the return to democracy, even though there have been no disappearances since Alfonsín took office. The reason for this increase is that the Mothers have involved other groups in their public protest. When the Mothers are not in the Plaza, they are still attending other gatherings, always fighting, learning, reflecting. They have learned to channel their anxiety and grief into constructive paths, and to invent new political strategies. These women are priestesses — they have come to symbolize the collective conscience of the country.

Nobody can pretend not to see them. Here they are in the bright afternoon light with their white kerchiefs and with the photographs of the disappeared hanging from ribbons around their tired necks. They are willing to use women's true and ineffable recourse in their battle: the body itself as a weapon, exposed, subjected to hunger strikes, to long marches, to all sorts of abuse, at times given over to torture. Students, workers and intellectuals have begun to join them in their demonstrations. On August 2, 1985, more than 80,000 persons joined a march convened by the Mothers, and wound through the centre of Buenos Aires, shouting their slogan: "Justice and punishment for the guilty".

Through the years, the Mothers have learned by necessity to be wary, patient and persistent, and that is the prevailing attitude even now that the much discredited military has been ousted and the popular, democratically elected Alfonsín is president. As one of Alfonsín's first official acts, he appointed a Commission, headed by the writer Ernesto Sábato, to inquire into the fate of the disappeared. The Commission's results are documented in the report called *Nunca Más* (Never Again) (CONADEP, 1984). The first trial has been held, in a civilian court, of the nine major leaders of the three Juntas; the prosecutor has asked for life sentences for some and shorter sentences for others. Some might think the Mothers should be satisfied. But few of them to date have learned the fate of their own children and grandchildren. The original search goes on; their original aims remain the same, that *all* the guilty be brought to justice. They are still asking for "Life for the disappeared and punishment for the guilty''. For this reason, the demonstrations of the Mothers of the Plaza de Mayo continue, even though the kidnapping, torture, killing, and imprisonment of innocent Argentineans has stopped under Alfonsín.

In the early years, the Mothers were called the "Madwomen of the Plaza de Mayo", an attempt by the generals and their cohorts to dismiss them and their claims, using the age-old technique of a male-dominated society by calling women regarded as "out of their place" crazy. As mothers, they were treated with certain deference; nevertheless, their attempts to locate their loved ones were seen as being insane actions, which diminished their importance in the eyes of the military. A few centuries ago no doubt they would have been denounced as witches. But these witches, or Madwomen, have survived, have stayed united in spite of all adversities and all divisive methods used against them, including infiltration, kidnapping, torture and murder of some of their members. One cannot detect in them any political discrepancies, nor any desires for power for power's sake. They are determined and courageous; they are witnesses who dared to speak the dreadful truth about the military government. I would like to insist once again that, for years, they acted alone. Not even the Catholic Church, as an institution, supported them, although individual clergy members did. They defied the traditional, patriarchal society as well as the military Junta when they went out into the street and became public figures, and showed themselves ready to accept all the risks implicit in such rebellious activity.

By their public actions, they have become important and influential in Latin American politics. They have learned to use old political techniques in new and dramatic ways. For instance, their silent and passive marches speak louder and more eloquently than any oration could.

At the present time, the Argentinean people find themselves staggered by the testimony of survivors being given in the courtrooms. And the Madwomen are now regarded as heroines because they defied the silence. They, themselves, see their work to be the same as ever — to continue to fight until the last criminal is brought to justice.

As I sit sobered by these thoughts, a woman approaches me. She tells me her parents were exterminated in Auschwitz and that her son, 30 years old, disappeared from the University of Buenos Aires. It does not help her that there is now democracy in Argentina. She is still afraid; she will always be afraid. She begs me not to use her name. How can one comprehend such misfortune? How can it be that this woman has now been a victim of two holocausts?

The House of the Mothers is located in Hipolito Irigoyen Street and was donated by the government of Holland. Other governments who might have helped them, such as the United States government, remained silent and offered no aid. When I visited the house, there was tremendous activity. The Mothers bustle about, putting up posters, organizing meetings, receiving visitors. Said one Mother, ''Here, there is much pain but much love''. The walls are covered with photographs of the disappeared. I notice that most are young, attractive, brimming with good health; there are many young women among them. I cannot help asking myself again, ''How can a civilized society descend to such a barbarous level?''

It is Thursday. We are all on our way to the plaza. I find myself walking beside Hebe Bonafini, President of the Mothers; she makes me feel tall and strong. I can think of nothing to say to her but we smile at one another. The women gather around the obelisk, greeting one another, embracing and kissing friends. I think of their sleepless nights. They arrange themselves for another march in favour of life, in defiance of death. They tell me that, while they are marching in the plaza, they feel very close to their children. They feel their children are by their sides. And the truth is, in the plaza where forgetting is not allowed, memory recovers its meaning. Cruelty of human beings to other human beings is judged. The devastation of the young, the workers, the students, the young pregnant women and the grandmothers is remembered, denounced, mourned, judged.

The activities of the Mothers have not changed since democratization in the sense that they continue to go to marches and there still is no answer for the disappearances of their children. The biggest change in the Mothers' group is the attempt to incorporate other human rights organizations in their plight and to pressure for more immediate answers.

Another Thursday in August in Buenos Aires. A conspiring sun caresses our skin. The plaza is full of life and movement: couples holding hands, old people enjoying the sun, children and pigeons. The Mothers arrive, immaculate, serene and disturbing in their white kerchiefs with the embroidered names and dates. Slowly, their healing aura spreads and creates a blue space in this plaza that is now theirs, that now has to belong to them. They form their sacred circle. Earlier, the world watched and supported them, but silent, fearful Argentina averted its eyes. Now the country joins them and weeps with them, because the Mothers fight not only for their own children but for all children. They are marching to win all rights due a free people, to make any violation of those rights unacceptable. The Mothers have a close acquaintance with death but they are completely committed to life.[7]

I wish to express special appreciation to Nora Feminia, to whom I also dedicate this work. She helped me get to know the Mothers and very generously shared her own work with me concerning women and politics in Argentina.

FOOTNOTES

1 The *dirty war* designates the epoch beginning before the overthrow of the dictator Juan Perón in 1975 until the restoration of democracy and the election of Raúl Alfonsín as President in 1984.

2 It is estimated that half of the total number of disappearances, involving approximately 5000 persons, occurred in 1976 during the first year of military rule. In 1979, another 35 percent disappeared and in 1978, 15 percent disappeared. Information obtained from the following study: Eduardo Duhalde. *El estado terroísta argentino* ("The Argentinean Terrorist State"). Madrid: Argos Vergara, 1983.

3 For further information, see:
Ronald Dworkin. "Report from Hell", *The New York Times Book Review*, Volume XXXIII, Number 12:11-14.

4 For a detailed account of the treatment of political prisoners, including testimony of survivors, see:

A Visit to the Mothers of the Plaza de Mayo

Ernesto Sábato, editor. National Commission of the Rights of People (CONADEP). *Nunca Más*
("Never Again"). Buenos Aires: Eudena, 1984.

5 Jean Pierre Bousquet. *Las Locas de la Plaza de Mayo*. Buenos Aires: El Cid, 1982, p. 43.

6 As of this writing in April of 1986, the nine military officers who governed Argentina through
three successive Juntas have been tried in a civilian court and sentenced. The leader of the three-
man junta, Videla, received a life sentence, as did Admiral Massera. Ex-president Viola received
a 17-year sentence, and ex-president Galtierei was absolved. There is bitterness at this verdict,
because, for the most part, the Mothers cannot accept a compromise for the guilty ones. This is
a point of contention between the Mothers and the Alfonsín regime.

7 There are various books concerning the Mothers; for example, see the following books of poetry:
Juan Gelman. *La Junta Luz*. Buenos Aires: Editorial Tierra Firme, 1985.
Vicente Zito Lema. *Mater*. Buenos Aires: Editorial Tierra Firme, 1985.
Also see:
John Simpson and Jana Bennett. *The Disappeared and the Mothers of the Plaza de Mayo*. New
York: St. Martin's Press, 1985.

REFERENCES

Bousquet, Jean Pierre. *Las Locas de la Plaza de Mayo*. Bueno Aires: El Cid, 1982.

Duhalde, Eduardo. *El estado terroísta argentino*. Madrid: Argos Vergara, 1983.

Sábato, Ernesto, ed. National Commission of the Rights of the People (CONADEP). *Nunca Más*.
Buenos Aires: Eudena, 1984.

The Grandmothers of the Plaza de Mayo

Fall seems to be children's favourite season. Fond of the colours that suggest magic, the shadows and the sound of puddles when they jump in those prohibited territories, they walk through this season as if through large carpets of leaves. Many save innocent scraps of yellow and crimson in their pockets full of inventions. They return home enchanted by nothing more than an autumn day. However, not all of them return to their true homes or to their true parents because they are the kidnapped children of the desaparecidos, the disappeared.

To a casual observer, children have little to do with the events that occurred in Argentina in 1975 during the so-called "Period of Process," when General Rafael Videla took power and ordered the arrest of all "subversives," that is to say, any person with different ideas. The armed forces of this purportedly civilized nation became a faithful reproduction of the German Nazis, whose main goal was the creation of a perfect Aryan race without the contamination of pluralistic thought. For this reason, the military's "process of national reconstruction" took on another name to the impotent spectators: the Dirty War. Because what is dirtier than making entire families disappear or abducting children either out of or still within the motherly womb?

Countries on both sides of the Atlantic Ocean have committed these crimes with absolute impunity. The populations of Germany and Argentina have contemplated with indifference the scene when Jews were forced onto the trains of death and when Ford Falcons without license plates drove through the streets of Buenos Aires swallowing up people like large, green lizards.

Amnesty International has affirmed that approximately 30,000 people disappeared in Argentina, among them children and pregnant women. The families of many of the missing have accepted the death of their loved ones, but not of their grandchildren. It would be more devastating to think that there are two generations of the disappeared: the generation of the parents and that of their children.

The Association of the Mothers of the Plaza de Mayo was established in 1976 with the goal of demanding justice with regard to their missing children. This group became the first public organization to demonstrate in an otherwise silent and frightened Argentina. Women still march in Buenos Aires each Thursday wearing their white kerchiefs embroidered with their children's names, celebrating the rituals of life, and defying death and the guilty persecutors.

Parallel to the organization of mothers, a group called the Grandmothers of the Plaza de Mayo was formed by fourteen grandmothers, later multiplied to almost 200. The central purpose of this organization was to search for the children who were born in concentration camps and who, in most cases, were kidnapped by their parents' torturers. Until now, 42 of almost 200 of these children known to live in Argentina have been found.

María Isabel de Mariani is the president of the Grandmothers of the Plaza de Mayo. Her eyes reflect all the tenderness and pain of our own grandmothers. She speaks calmly, with a dignity that only seems possible from one who has suffered so much. María Isabel states that her purpose is to try to find all of these children so they can be returned to their true families and so that they do not live with the assassins of their biological parents.

There are various methods used to obtain information about these small children. A few sources exist that document the birth of children in prison. In addition, there are oral resources, people who advise the Grandmothers of the Plaza de Mayo when a child suddenly appears in the home of a family previously without children. To infiltrate these homes and obtain the necessary information, the grandmothers themselves work as maids or the grandfathers as plumbers.

The association periodically publishes photographs of the missing children in the country's newspapers. Thanks to this visible information, the Argentinean public, previously silent, has' responded. Once a child is found, a judge demands that his or her identity be confirmed. The grandmothers have already resolved this problem. They have initiated research to develop a technique of genetic analysis that does not involve the parents, but the extended family to verify the children's true identity. Once this is determined, the child is examined by psychologists and psychiatrists so she or he will not suffer any type of trauma, and so the return to her or his real family will be full of happiness and tranquillity.

The Grandmothers of the Plaza de Mayo represent another form of political action within a clearly female imagery. They search for a new generation of Argentineans knowing that the valuable youths of the first generation lost their lives in clandestine prisons or were thrown into the sea from helicopters. María Isabel de Mariani and other representatives of the association travel throughout the world telling their stories. They talk about their endless work, especially in the beginning when they searched for their children and grandchildren twenty-four hours a day. This search has involved their dual roles as mothers and grandmothers.

When the grandmothers speak, they do not speak with hatred but with eloquence. They are determined to find the children, either their own or someone else's grandchildren. Individual desires do not emerge here, because this search has become a collective effort.

At times, I imagine the women in the parks on autumn days, looking at the children in their multi-coloured jackets as they make piles of leaves that they will later jump into, waves of sound. Other times, I think of them knitting wool booties for the crude winters, because somehow those small and innocent children will return. They are grandmothers like all grandmothers, and for this reason, their search is our own.

Thanks to the steps taken by the Grandmothers of the Plaza de Mayo, techniques have been perfected for recovering missing children that are in the homes of other families throughout the world. The symbol of the Grandmothers is the same as that of the Mothers of the Plaza de Mayo: a white kerchief saying "Identity, Justice and Liberty."

I think that, one day, the Plaza de Mayo will be full of mothers, grandmothers and small children playing with the pigeons, and the kerchiefs will float up into the immense sky. Fortunately, such a sinister official policy involving the disappearance of children has only existed in Argentina. We must work together so that this will never happen again. The grandmothers of the Plaza de Mayo are ours. We cannot forget. Someday, we could also be them.

Isla Negra

*And even if they blindfolded my bleeding eyes, even
if the sweet, dreaded knives approached my eyes'
illuminated pupils, even then I would know that
I was arriving at my home, approaching Isla Negra
near the sea.*

On the island, when I was five years old, my mother, with her
coppery hair and eyes of clear water, told me: "In this place,
you have the universe: the tender yet defiant rocks, the
tempestuous sea with its majestic delicacy, and all of the earth's
honeysuckles." I was happy with these gifts and certainties, safe
and triumphant with my pockets full of sunshine. Now, among
my pains and dead children, I search for myself, feeling
shipwrecked in the mirrors of fear, and always I see my mother's
copper hair approach and my pockets peek out into the sunlight.

I gained this wisdom, these scraps of life, as a legacy of Isla
Negra, the same Isla Negra loved by Pablo Neruda and many
others. The island is not an island, nor is it black; it is a fishing
cove seventy kilometres north of Santiago.

No one knows the story behind the strange name, but
perhaps that is part of its enchantment. In the 1930s, Pablo
Neruda began to build a house dangling from the sky and sea.
Little by little, he constructed wooden rooms and open stars
falling from the heavens. He filled Isla Negra with figureheads
and mysterious shells that still contained the sounds of the ocean
in their corollas.

To grow up in Isla Negra, to walk on the fresh, dirt paths,
to lose oneself in the vegetable gardens and, more than anything,
to learn to spend time in its pure and imaginative dimension, were
and continue to be, the most heartfelt legacies of this territory
near the sea.

Isla Negra is characterized by a coastline bordered by pre-
cipices. The town's women are tied to the earth; they have faces
of bread and are good people. There are also embroiderers in Isla

Negra, people who resemble the territory that surrounds them. They are discreet in their dress, and have a slow and sure step.

Nevertheless, when the embroiderers display their works, all of the island's splendour — the unrestrained ocean, the sand full of agate, the chickens running crazy through the fields, the sunsets — all of nature and those gifts in my pocket acquire an incredibly beautiful effect. This is Isla Negra, *this is our island*, this is the island where lovers return to renew their promises, the island of dreams and of good and bad love. One returns to the island like the tides, inseparable from the sunsets and the captivating odours of the flowers that besiege the coast.

Light falls and scatters on the beach in an astounding litany that reminds me of small necklaces of birds unfastening across the wide sky. One can distinguish couples hand in hand, kissing next to the angry sea that also responds with a growing, painful embrace. In the distance, one can see couples in front of Pablo Neruda's house, reciting "Poem 20" or "The Song of Despair."

Pablo Neruda's house has not been converted into the sanctuary of love and freedom. It hurts my soul to see this house, suspended from the sky, full of bells, yellow flowers and figureheads, empty, closed by military authorities. A huge sign attached to a tree states, "House closed: visitors not permitted." Nevertheless, many have visited this house since Neruda's death in September, 1973, twenty-one days after the military coup d'etat.

On the fine, wooden fence that surrounds the house, pilgrims have inscribed love messages, things like, "Pablo will always live among us," "Help us, Pablo," and "Chile lives." They will never be able to close this house, because it would be impossible to close the sounds of the ocean or the bells that give birth to the wind's song, or to exterminate the agate in the sand.

I wander through the leafy, eucalyptus forests that form part of the area's strange geography. The odour permeates all of my body's pores and the roar of the sea constantly caresses me. I am happy. I remember daily walks with a man I loved. Through that love, I learned to stroll through the invisible mirrors of Isla

Negra. I still look at myself in them and, between the thresholds of the vigil, I see myself.

He is still alive; I think he will never die. He is forty years older than I, his hair is a giant pillow of white knowledge and eroticism. He brought me to Isla Negra one day. We purposely got lost to find ourselves in the forest. He invited me to his house, to his rooms full of music and pain. I remained in his house far from the sea but close to the eucalyptus groves for many years. We stayed close to each other every summer, speaking in silence, laughing at times, carrying on discussions that were dominated by his vanity, so typical of older men who have achieved success too late in life.

Even now we love each other, and Isla Negra reminds me of his warm hands, always generous and ready to hold mine because love in solitude was a small knife scraping me. Nights on Isla Negra remind me of warm wine, grapes at midnight and his feet as generous as his hands. Those large hands washed my hair and helped me to dry it with towels mixed with the scent of eucalyptus.

I continue through a small garden and come upon Teresita, the town mystic, caring for her beautiful vegetables. Teresita has two teeth from so much laughing, and her face, whipped by the ocean winds, bears a glowing vigour. She is one of the oldest embroiderers and, through her works, she transmits the pains of the sky and hell, the agonies of the soul as well as the love of God. She tells me that her ideas come to her in dreams, and at dawn while her husband, Joaquín, snores, she translates these brilliant colours into cloth.

Yesterday, she told me that she saw her radiant mother in the veil of a nebulous dream, who told her: "Tere, Tere, I am here." She said that her mother had been very beautiful, all dressed in white as if for her first communion. Teresita elaborated on how the visit from her dead mother would appear in her work. She said she wants to use a lot of yellow so her mother will shine in her white dress.

I say goodbye to Teresita. I cross another stone road until I arrive at Eudovijes' house, who always has a dining room full of hungry people although she does not always have something to serve. Nevertheless, she finds potatoes, cabbage, chicken and fresh eggs for the passersby, the vagabonds and the starving who she collects and celebrates, showering them with food.

It becomes dark and clear in Isla Negra as the sky begins to get drowsy in yellow and orange. The sea, after those intense, shifting flights that touch the knees of the passersby, retires to lull the inhabitants of the island and the couples who make love in rooms facing the sea. As I descend the stone road, the fireflies bloom around yellow flowers. I approach the ocean so I can also shelter myself with the gentleness of the tide.

At dusk, the sky takes on the shapes of larks and butterflies. I approach the sea, and a great silence seizes the spectacular afternoon. Lovers hold hands and light candles by Don Pablo's house. As they ask for eternal love, a light, I do not know if it is a distant lighthouse or Don Pablo's room that blinks and illuminates.

This empty house with the sign that says "Visitors not permitted" remains open for those who can still see with their hearts. I head up the hill towards the house far from the sea and, although the hands of the man I loved in Isla Negra have shrunk, and desperation has chilled the candour of his feet, he waits for me. His hands begin to wash my hair, to dry it with eucalyptus branches, to heat wine.

Today, no one has died in Isla Negra, and everyone has opened their houses. Today, we have all returned and Teresita dreams of us and embroiders us in a shining tapestry.

Alaide Foppa:
She Will Not Be Forgotten
For Alba Guzmán

To disappear, to cease to exist as if by a diabolical magic act, has already become a daily occurrence under the authoritarian governments of Latin America. Curiously, in 1966, Guatemala initiated this monstrous system that erases every trace of life of the missing person. During the Second World War, the Nazis preserved traces of thousands of victims assassinated in the gas chambers or dead from fear and pain. Nevertheless, the Latin American militaries have been either very skillful or very sinister by erasing every sign of the lost being.[1]

The Latin American woman writer suffers a fate similar to that of the disappeared. Many times, she is alive but no one knows that she exists and her writings, considered to be lightweight, shapeless, womanly things, pass into the annals of oblivion.

Alaide Foppa suffers from this double disappearance. First, she disappeared in Guatemala in December of 1980, and not a trace of her has been found. Foppa represents the inherited destiny of the woman writer who disappears, who evaporates in the physical, real plane as she does in the plane of her writings. Despite the tremendous importance of Alaide as a founder of and assiduous collaborator on the magazine *Fem*[2] and the excellence of her poetic work, Foppa is disappearing from readings and classrooms, but not from the memory of those who knew her.

This short piece attempts to rescue Alaide Foppa from oblivion, to situate her within a solid cultural context in the hope that, in the future, her work will be re-evaluated and will begin to be read within the appropriate canon.

My interest in Alaide Foppa began thanks to Alba Guzmán, an educator and the current director of a program on the education of indigenous women. Alba constantly mentioned Alaide and her sober, profound way of telling transcendental truths about the exploitation of indigenous people and, in particular, of indigenous Guatemalan women. Alaide also represented a model for the women of her own class.

Born in Italy in 1936 in the lap of a bourgeois family, Alaide was raised in Europe and on Guatemalan ranches. She learned to understand her privileged situation, and transferred her worries to indigenous and marginal people, especially women. Foppa settled in Mexico for approximately twenty years, and again in the 1970s. She and her husband, Alfonso Solorzano, a Guatemalan politician, both left Guatemala for political reasons. Nevertheless, during the entire period of exile in Mexico, Alaide often returned to her beloved Guatemala, until the last time in December 1980 when she and her driver were kidnapped as she left her home.

Foppa was incredibly active in Mexico: she taught courses in Italian Literature at the School of Humanities of U.S.A.C., and began a radio program in Mexico City in the 1970s called Women's Forum. Alaide was one of the first to raise the consciousness of middle-class women by presenting in her forum numerous interviews with maids, indigenous women and herbalists.

Alaide Foppa's most interesting writings are her essays on the condition of women. They represent pioneering works for Mexico in the 1970s, and constitute foundations of thought and ideology on the status of Latin American women. Foppa's more outstanding essays include: "Anatomy is Not Destiny," "Salary for Domestic Work," "Of Herbs and Herbalists" and "The Place of Maids."[3] Foppa's style as an essayist is agile, pleasant and inquisitive. She questions, invades, and returns to ancient history as in her essay, "Anatomy is not Destiny," where she refers to the function of women in society from Biblical times to the present. She demonstrates that, in the past, a woman's body existed only for procreation; therefore she had to dedicate all of her attention to it.

The comments that Foppa makes about the menstrual flow and its negative associations are revealing. From the time of the

Levites, when women had to isolate themselves for seven days, menstruation has been considered "dirty." The same characterization has been made of maternity; in many societies, a woman isolated herself for seven days if she gave birth to a girl. The essay continues to make parallels between the roles of women that relegate her to inferiority, and examines the different ways that biology is used in a patriarchal society to marginalize women. Again, at the time they were published, these essays represented radical openings in a society where women still were not permitted to think about their anatomy, much less their destiny.

"Of Herbs and Herbalists" is a magnificent interview with two herbalists from a town in the outer regions of Mexico called Amatlán. Through this interview, where Foppa never acts as an intruder, but rather as a mere observer anxious to learn, the reader learns about the tradition of the herbalists, so typically female and so typically Latin American. The mystery of this popular knowledge is unmasked and converted into a vital, daily activity. Foppa says: "I thought I would discover secrets, would approach what they call popular knowledge, and I encountered a simple, dry woman who carried out her job without any mystery, who helped people however she could. Later, I found out — she did not tell me herself — that Vicenta organized a small hospital of four rooms in Amatlán" (*Fem4*, May-June 1980, p. 52).

Along with her work as an essayist, which embraced a varied gamut of topics, Alaide Foppa wrote five books of poetry: *La sin ventura* ("The Luckless Woman"), *Los dedos de mi mano* ("My Fingers"), *Aunque es de noche* ("Although it is Nighttime"), *Guirnalda de primavera* ("Garland of Spring"), *Elogio de mi cuerpo* ("Praise of my Body") and *Las palabras y el tiempo* ("Words and Time").[4] These poems were compiled into one edition that was edited and completed by her mother in .1982.

A careful reading of Foppa's poetry points to women's inherited destiny; women are the central theme of her works and, at times, an obsessive motive. Her best known book, *Los dedos de mi mano* ("My Fingers"), is dedicated exclusively to the theme of maternity as complete surrender but also as limitation, as in the second poem of the collection, which is untitled: Clear light of morning / I wish for your eyes / softness of early grass / for your hair / and in your chest heart of flame. Oh who would be able / to sew in your soul a garden / But I am only / your blind transitory dwelling (p. 126). This book of poems also expresses feelings of uneasiness, as in the following verse: I will be able to allow myself to be injured again / but today mister / remove from my side / the things that hurt me (p. 128).

Foppa's poetry revolves around women and, in particular, around the image of the woman who waits, the woman who, although not yet free, yearns for a better destiny. In a later poetic work, entitled *Elogio de mi cuerpo* ("Praise of my Body"), Foppa celebrates and exalts the feminine. These poems are epigrammatic, marking a radical change from her previous poetry, full of images and metaphors. Alaide talks about the mouth, the breasts, the waist, the genitalia, never with a narcissistic tone but rather, in a delicate and precise fashion, as in the poem entitled "Mouth": Where the tongue / light serpent of delight / undulates softly / and shelters the miracle of the word (p. 33).

Alaide Foppa's last book, *Las palabras y el tiempo* ("Words and Time"), is her most profound and philosophical work. Now with a mature voice and a style that is always more synthetic and precise, the poet goes in search of the unities of body-spirit and life-death. Above all, Foppa searches for a more transcendental communication. Alaide's best known poem is called "Woman," (p. 81) presented here in its entirety:

A being that does not stop being
Not the remote artificial rose
of which the poets sing
Not the wicked witch that
the inquisitors burned
Not the feared and desired prostitute.
Not the blessed mother
Not the withered and mocked spinster

Not the one obliged to be good
Not the one obliged to be bad
Not the one that lives
because they let her live
Not the one that must always
say yes
A being that tries to
know who it is
and that begins to exist.

The essential purpose of this short essay is to make Alaide Foppa appear, to return her to life so that her figure will not belong only to a cult of ghosts. It is important that future studies reconstruct her life, since so little is known about her, that her formation under the care of indigenous nannies be discussed, that her feminist political ideology be studied and above all, that her poetic work be rescued.

It is difficult to find Alaide Foppa and it seems that only the magazine *Fem* remembers her constantly. Her name is overlooked in anthologies of Latin American poetry and her essays are not mentioned. Alaide Foppa does not only represent a missing woman writer but also an important political figure of Latin American feminism. She deserves to appear, she deserves to be read.

FOOTNOTES

1 For more information about disappearances in Latin America see the reports of Amnesty International for the respective countries.

2 The magazine *Fem*, one of the oldest feminist magazines in Latin America, was founded by Alaide Foppa and others in 1970.

3 Foppa's principal and most accessible articles are:

"Of Herbs and Herbalists". *Fem* 4-14, May-June 1980, pp. 51-53.

"What Women Write". *Fem* 3-10, January-October 1979, pp. 5-7.

"Anatomy is not Destiny". *Fem* 2-1, October-December 1976, pp. 8-13.

"Daughters — Mothers — Daughters Mothers". *Fem* 3-9, October-December 1978, pp. 5-6.

4 This edition was published by Servimensa Centroamericana, Guatemala City. All of the references correspond to this edition, published in 1986, since all previous editions are out-of-print.

Delfina Nahuenhual

Her name was Delfina, and when she had just arrived at our house, I thought she had been stranded by a little fishing boat, or that she possessed powers to see beneath the water. I was mistaken and correct in all of my suppositions. It is true that Delfina came on a small boat from a black island plagued by the insomnia of its exiled inhabitants, from a town slowly consuming its own past. She was an Araucanian from the most remote Araucanians, and her name was that of a princess or a queen; it was a testimony to indomitable places. But more than anything, Delfina smelled of the sea, and I always saw her as being blue like peace or a small starfish.

Delfina Nahuenhual was my nanny, my mama, my prophet, the mother of my soul. She was the woman who raised the Latin American bourgeoisie. We all had a mama in addition to our real mama who greeted us cheerfully in the morning and did not see us again until after dark. Our nanny was the one who cared for sick little girls, the one who was our companion, the one who cured us from lovesickness with herbs.

I was not exactly a bourgeois daughter because my parents were not bourgeois. For this reason, Delfina was not a mere servant but a knot of secrets and prophecies. From her, I learned that wounds could be cured by making small crosses on my knees, and that, merely by liking someone, we could manage to make them like us too. My nanny wore enormous, wool shawls, and like her name, her scents seemed to be part of a geography more marine than earthly. She smelled of the wind and distance. To cure the pains of spasms, she used to ceremoniously stick small eucalyptus branches and ground up cigarette butts on her forehead.

My sister and I used to dress up in Delfina's shawl, which was her most prized possession, since she lost her scant fortune in the unforgettable earthquake in the potters' zones of Chillán. Delfina Nahuenhual then rode a wild mule to the capital city to search for a job as a servant, but for us, she was our mama, a vulnerable and generous woman who believed in goblins, the miracles of the Virgin of Carmen and mirrors paved with omens.

I did not invent my Delfina's magic, nor do I present her from an anthropological viewpoint. I merely think she was born a believer, that she smelled like delicate lies and that her hands seemed to predict the results of inspirations. In my country, magic molds us because we are very poor and falsely religious. We endlessly repeat "God willing" but at times, God is not willing, and whips us with earthquakes and chains of hunger. However, God might be willing, so, like Delfina, we continue to practice this pure credulity of believers or dreamers.

Delfina, a shaman at the feet of a foul-smelling stove, told stories that she made up as she went along between the sips of *mate* that we all shared. We secretly entered fables and graveyards, and the night seemed darker and scarier while she attacked us with those deliciously frightful nightmares. Little by little, Delfina convinced us to enter her prodigious dream. Then, with the delicate movement of wings, she would say good-night and go to her small part of the kitchen, cold from the surrounding china, until the following morning.

My greatest concern was to see her in this room so far from the rest of us, plagued by the odours of the kitchen. She was accompanied by pots and pans even at night. The roof of her room leaked, and she used a clay pot to collect the water running from the heavens.

Not only her room held a feeling of absence. At meal times, my sister and I felt the separation of plates and knives. Delfina, colour of fish, skin of peaches, left the dining room and joined the embers in the poor, little kitchen. She occupied her habitat, the territory of poor women and we, the future society ladies, ate alone, distant from the smell of the poor.

My Delfina, why didn't we invite you to share our table? Why did we only allow your servant's hands to pass us the salt and pepper? Why didn't you cover us with stories at lunchtime, and only dare to tell us of the south winds and the little spirits at night by candle when you sat at the foot of our bed while your shawl gave us all the smoke and heat of your country?

When I nestle on Delfina's chest today, she smells of herbs and solitude. I still go to her room. We tell stories; we are accomplices, inhabitants of similar and different bodies and destinies. I tell her about my dislikes, my bleedings, my dead babies. My nanny's womb is also a dry crystal made from alien children, from alien babies. Delfina shows me her photographs. All the little girls she raised, the little girls she never had, the first communions that she watched from the bannister.

My nanny is more than seventy-years old. She lives in a borrowed room and saves photographs of borrowed, little girls in a dresser, of those girls who ate in the dining room in the ceremonies of separate knives and tables.

Disappearance: A Devil's Trick

Children are fascinated by magic tricks. They love to watch multi-coloured handkerchiefs appear and disappear, or a white rabbit being plucked from a black hat. At times, to disappear seems no more than a vanishing act, a magic trick performed at birthday celebrations. Tragically, in reality, very few of the disappeared return. Their relatives are left alone to try to bring back the dead, buried in the prime of life.

I deliberately begin this sinister tale with a metaphor of childhood innocence. Children may be believers who enjoy an older person's tricks, but these same children, when confronted with grave and Mephistophelean disappearances, dare to question and fearlessly approach evil. Adults often refuse to enter such diabolic territory.

In authoritarian regimes, things do not disappear — people do. In speaking of them, one has two choices: passive silence, which implies giving in to fear, or a denial of silence, oblivion. The second choice implies an explicit denunciation, a search, and, many times, death, for those who dare to retrieve the memory or the body of a loved one.

The seekers are women and children, children not yet dominated by the reserve and caution of adults. Their natural curiosity makes them more suited to the search. It is they who can play hide-and-seek, hoping only to find one another.

Adults who dare to participate in the labyrinthine process of finding the disappeared run the risk of losing their own lives. Nevertheless, adults and relatives of the disappeared appeal to tribunals, protest, and participate in non-violent demonstrations. They play a dangerous game, refusing to accept the culture of death, wanting only to celebrate the culture of life.

Fearless children can get close to evil, to the sinister — thus their ambivalent fascination with horror movies, the bogeyman, and playing in the dark. Children play "Pin the Tail on the Donkey" blindfolded; the disappeared look like they're playing the game, but their eyes are burned, not bound — the playful turns sinister. The child who gets close to and plays with evil is motivated by an instinct to know and to understand. The adult fears the sinister, the dreadful, and opts for not knowing, not seeing.

These comments are based on my several years of giving talks about torture and the disappeared. Many times my audience is stupified, mute. A timid collective consciousness exists when it comes to asking why civilized countries practice such techniques of horror. A concrete example can be found in the German people, who swore so many times they knew nothing about the existence of concentration camps next door to their villages and towns.

Adults opt for an easy silence, a silence of cowards. At times, they choose to blame the victim: "That's what happens when you get involved in bad things." Children ask the executioner, "Why do the police take their own people away?" And in this honest question lies a very profound dilemma: the disappearances are executed by people of the same country, the same city. The disappeared do not vanish because of outside forces. It is possible that the people responsible later frequent the same cafés as the victims' families, that the executioners' and the victims' children attend the same school.

Children ask not only "Where is he/she?" but also "How is he?" It is not unusual to hear them asking or worrying about what the disappeared get to eat, how they sleep, what kind of quarters they're in. Children, too, are concerned about basic human rights, bread and a roof overhead.

Frequently, children ask what clothes the disappeared were wearing, and the children whose fathers and mothers have disappeared return again and again to the place from which they vanished, or to the place where they remember having played with their relatives. The parks, the plazas, are converted into symbols of loss and absence. Children re-live these diabolic scenes as part of their everyday lives, now fragmented.

To disappear is to become no more than a dead soul in life. It is also to engulf loved ones in a permanent question, "Where could they be?'' The proof that the disappeared are no invention is not a relative or other survivor who returns. Rather, it is the number of illuminators, fighters, who go out in search, who remember obsessively the missing, who celebrate their birthdays and even the anniversaries of their disappearances.

Children, those who ask and those who know, suffer whether they are direct victims of disappearances or have simply had to accept that, unlike the white rabbit in the magician's hat, the disappeared do not often reappear. Thus their desire to touch the cases of the disappeared, to verify the truth. Thus their questions about whether I have had relatives who vanished. In the personal resides a political question.

To talk about the disappeared is not only to challenge oblivion. It is also to make sure this never happens again, and to learn not to forget. Children realize that to know these stories is the beginning of truth — a realization shared by the women who dare not ask simply for their own children, but for all. Disappearances in Latin America cannot be compared to the magic tricks that parade across a stage. The disappeared almost never return: all the more reason for the appeared to speak out about them. The more the appeared defy the conspiracy of silence, the more disappeared we will find.

The Generals' Bonfires
The Death of Rodrigo Rojas in Chile

The clarity of certain autumn days allows the passerby, distracting him or herself wandering through the park, to discover the outlines of constellations in the leaves that are scattered on the lawn by an ordered fate. The unique, separate leaves resemble fans of intermittent colours to the observer, who, overwhelmed by the colours, is unaware of invading the certain, yet seldom, pondered perfection.

In autumn, the images of the people who collect the leaves, and clean and sweep the streets, reflect a preoccupation with order and disorder in the cities. It is a common portrait: a man kneeling and gathering a dense collection of leaves in the state parks. One can also observe the same man methodically burning the leaves, erasing all signs of the intrepid and unequalled autumn.

The stubbornness in the sweeping and cleaning of streets, the cleaning of the city's walls, in the imposition of order, is a characteristic of governments that repress, torture, and behead. This obsessive need to preserve the rigidity that surrounds humans stems from a desire to control. To control everything, including the radiant reds, the browns and violets of fall. In this way, military governments attempt to control even the impetuous order of nature.

The government of Augusto Pinochet has taken on the responsibility of cleaning my city, Santiago, Chile, an enchanting place surrounded by wild necklaces of mountains that reflect changing scenarios according to the direction of the clouds or the rebirth of the snow caps. This tyrant has said: "In Chile, a leaf cannot drop without me hearing it." In Santiago, the leaves have disappeared, as children disappear when they go to buy bread, and as adults disappear while sleeping, taken from their books and their children, never to return to their homes, or to their relatives and friends.

I weave these images of fall in all of its splendour, but I cannot stop thinking that, just as they burn leaves in Santiago, they also burn people. Here, I am not referring to a scene in a horror movie, but to a specific, sinister event that took place in Santiago on July 2, 1986.

Scenes of fire have become commonplace in Santiago. At the beginning of 1973, Pinochet's forces burned 'subversive' books in public bonfires in the city's neighbourhoods. Many cautious and fearful individuals resolved to burn their own books. Santiago became a painful bonfire in a castrating hell where words were devoured by a crazy fever to clean up 'subversive' thoughts.

In this same way, witches were burned from the 11th to the 14th centuries. The public nature of the punishment was as important as the burning itself. It was important for people to see the hair and the eyes of the women who were engulfed in the flames, illuminated for being alien to the discourses of power, for curing sick people, for saving lives. Many healers of the Middle Ages were burned for knowing more than the medical doctors, just as many Jews were burned in the ovens of Auschwitz for being different, for being born Jewish.

Rodrigo Rojas was not a witch or a Jew, but a curious adolescent, and for this reason, in the Chile of Pinochet, he suffered the unjust and inhuman punishment of witches and Jews. I did not know Rodrigo, but I can imagine him as he burned in the bonfires. Perhaps he looked a bit like my brother, each of them exiled from his country, speaking a foreign language and desperately trying to learn more about his origins in anticipation of a possible return or to reconcile himself with the thought of not returning.

Rodrigo Rojas resembled many of my students. He was a photographer and liked to explore, to examine, to analyze images. Rodrigo Rojas was a little like all of us. Perhaps for this reason, his death brings us closer to him and also makes us fear our own possible destinies.

During his trip back to Chile, the nineteen-year old Rodrigo flew over rivers, peaks, and indomitable mountain ranges. He never knew that this trip marked the beginning of his death, because death arrives imprecisely, dominantly. It is almost impossible to reconcile oneself with the fact that death never misses a date. For this reason, death played a dirty trick on Rodrigo Rojas.

As with all exiles who return to their countries, Rodrigo Rojas spent days and months discovering that the majestic place he had idealized through a forgetful nostalgia was already another world. Rodrigo tried to recall the streets of his city. He travelled through the peripheral neighbourhoods. Perhaps he wanted to photograph hunger, but he ended up photographing and crucifying himself, caught up in the flames.

This fateful July 2, the Chilean police arrested Rojas and another youth, nineteen-year old Gloria Quintana. These two teenagers met in the middle of a student demonstration, and fate chose Rodrigo Rojas and Gloria Quintana. After severely mistreating Rojas and Quintana, it was not enough for the police to see them stripped and humiliated beyond pain and hatred. The police set them on fire, as in the German concentration camps where twelve million Jews, gypsies, communists, homosexuals and others died; as witches were burned in public places; as the Armenians were massacred; as African children, stomachs swollen with the burning of hunger, perish.

Rodrigo Rojas was *burned alive*. The horror of this scene lies in this phrase that cuts through us like a knife. The Chilean police, composed of fathers, husbands, brothers, and sons, burned a nineteen-year old boy. The usual question is "Why did they burn them?" or "What were the teenagers doing?" But within this question lies a fallacy. Why, when or what Rodrigo Rojas and Gloria Quintana were doing does not matter; only the truth matters — Rodrigo Rojas was killed by being burned alive.

The story of Rodrigo Rojas forms part of so many scenes of horror that have occurred under the Pinochet dictatorship. The wounded, embattled Chilean citizens did not go crazy when they learned of the events that took place in that Dantésque fire. The fascist press tried to cover up the event, but since Rodrigo

Rojas was a U.S. citizen, it was made public. How many other Rodrigos have there been in Chile? How many more will there be? How many young girls have died buying bread? How many mothers have seen their newly-born babies die in prison from fright?

It is no longer possible to silence Rodrigo Rojas. This curious, creative adolescent was not silent in life and will not be in death. The country talks about the "burned one," and everyone thinks about his body dissolving among the flames in useless agony. Rodrigo's double, Gloria Quintana, did not die, but is badly burned, her face disfigured and her eyes lost. No one will love Gloria Quintana, she will not have boyfriends or children. Gloria Quintana, with her face split and shapeless, will remind us that Rodrigo Rojas is alive.

Autumn reminds me of the bonfires of my country, of the blue bonfires where my grandmothers with singed hair cried out. I submerge myself in dreams full of pain. My fingertips, my hands, the sounds, all hurt, and I think that Rodrigo Rojas will not remain absent. He will approach our homes at dinnertime, his presence will remind us of chimneys and ovens. His spirit will wander, keep watch of our consciences. He will appear in the dreams of the people who burned him, not to seek vengeance, not to hate his captors, but to obligate them to look at him with his fine skin turned into a hide, blue with pain.

Rodrigo Rojas has not died. They have burned Rodrigo Rojas.

Alicia Was Not in Wonderland

Alicia Partnoy could have been one of us; could we have been Alicia? Here, I am not talking about Alice-in-Wonderland, the one who travelled through a magic looking-glass and discovered the secrets of innocence and nostalgia.

Our Alicia is also a traveller, but more than anything, a survivor who was confined in the putrid looking-glass of death and fear. Alicia was one of many young Argentineans who became part of the sinister and machiavellian invention of fascist governments: disappearances.

In January, 1977, Alicia Partnoy was imprisoned. She was released, or better said, reappeared in 1979, thanks to pressure from international human rights groups. How Alicia Partnoy reappeared and why the death squads allowed her to live are mysterious questions left to the benevolence of fate and good spirits. Partnoy's book, *The Little School*, is, according to her, a tribute to those who survived through memories of their loved ones and to the anonymous corpses, defeated and murdered, in Argentinean prisons. The book's title is the euphemism used to refer to the prison where Argentine citizens were held, tortured and executed.

Through writing, one may be able to exercise pain and neglect, but not torture, because the inexplicable wires that dispassionately launch electrical currents through the bodies of delirious victims cannot be translated into words. What can be put into writing is the fact that the most common elements are the most desired: the aroma of bread and coffee, and the promise of a soft drink on a prisoner's birthday.

In *The Little School*, Alicia Partnoy recreates with magical lyricism a mosaic of scenes from life in prison; for example, when the guards repented and decided to give the prisoner certain privileges:

They didn't bring me the soda that the fat visitor promised, but just because tóday is my birthday, they let me sit down on my bunk bed. I was surprised that they allowed me to sit because, according to Turco, this room is used to keep those of us with a record of bad behaviour, those who have refused to collaborate (p. 35).

In other scenes in *The Little School*, the protagonist only wants to remember her name, because by naming herself, she proves to herself that she is still alive, that she has not been lost in the Cardex file of people who have disappeared permanently. The soldiers use the tactic of referring to the prisoners by numbers, because a name, even if it is used by a torturer, invokes memories of the voices of mothers, brothers, sisters and teachers, and they know that memory is a powerful tool for survival.

At the Little School, I don't have a last name. Only Vasca calls me by my name. The guards have repeatedly said that numbers will be used to call us, but so far that has been just a threat. Since that moment, they have called me "Death." Maybe that is why, every day when I wake up, I say to myself that I, Alicia Partnoy, am still alive (p. 43).

At times, memory, the apprehension of a runaway illusion, becomes a fruitless way to continue and survive. When Alicia desperately tries to remember the face of her small daughter, Ruth, her body and memory protect her; they are selective and do not allow her to reconstruct this beloved face, shaped by an angelic innocence that becomes a howl of pain:

For a while now, I've been trying to recall Ruth's face. I can remember her big eyes, her almost non-existent little nose, the shape of her mouth. I recall the texture of her hair, the warmth of her skin. When I try to put it all together, something goes wrong. I just can't remember my daughter's face.

It has been two months since I've seen her. I want to believe that she is safe (p. 77).

In other instances, Alicia Partnoy returns to things that occurred many times in the past as unnoticed acts. She returns to the smell of bread or her mother's room filled with paintings. It is as if she is visiting from her cell, and all of the smells of her life return to her:

> *I made my third attempt at telepathy this afternoon. I used another method. I tried to imagine my parent's house on Uruguay Street, my mother and her paintings in the small back room, my father making tea in the kitchen, my brother bent over a book. The sunlight ... the trees in the backyard. I am okay, I repeated in my mind, I am alive, I am alive, still alive (p. 50).*

The smell of rain and the feeling of cleanliness that pure and refreshing air brings is also captured by the prisoner in her cell. The water that penetrates and dampens her is one of the signs that she is still alive: "This day had been different: the rain had made it different. Shortly after lunch, it had begun to rain. The smell of damp earth made her come to grips with the fact that she was still alive."

The smell of fresh bread also becomes a certainty and possibility of feeling alive in the prison of the living dead. In the section "Bread" Partnoy recreates all the different instances where bread became something marvellous and exquisite, as when crumbs were shared by some of the prisoners or when the guards took pity on them and instead of giving them one ration of bread, gave them two.

The Little School does not speak about the graphic horrors of torture, or of the abominable techniques used to obtain information from gagged prisoners. Through this text, Alicia Partnoy weaves feelings and motives, and communicates to us, for example, how the prisoners feel when they are allowed to touch each other, reaffirming themselves in the insane darkness, and what they felt when sharing a few crumbs of bread.

The reader is completely immersed in life in a cell, and feels as if she or he has travelled through the looking glass of this "Alice" who names herself so she will not forget, so she will always remember those who have died and those who have survived. For this reason, the final appendix is more chilling than any literary manifesto, because here Partnoy talks of people who existed, babies born in prison that were taken away by the same jailers who helped them to be born.

In these testimonies that are so graphic and chilling in their absolute truth, *The Little School* becomes alive and is filled with voices. We almost see Graciela or little Adrianita, just an infant. We almost hear the steps of Bruja taking the prisoners to the baths. We learn to hear the screams of torture at night, when Alicia says they will not convert her into an animal. Literature and the written word do not live in vain when the job of telling and recounting becomes a gesture of open arms, when the reader wants to embrace the characters in a book and tell them, "Don't worry anymore, you are not alone, I am here, I will write about you, I will read about you, I will remember you."

All of the quotations in this text are from The Little School *by Alicia Partnoy, published by Cleis, Pittsburgh, PA, 1987.*

Women Artists in Chile:
The Conscience of a Country in Crisis

A woman draws crosses on the pavement in defiance of traffic laws and the government's authority. Little by little, the cities, highways and roads fill with the crosses she creates. Sometimes, these drawings bear a strange message: "Peace for Sebastián Acevedo, a man who sacrificed himself in 1979 in front of a mesmerized crowd for wanting to know the whereabouts of his two children."

This unusual woman, Lotti Rosenfeld, is one of the many individuals in Chile today who defy the authoritarianism of Augusto Pinochet by means of a unique art full of social significance, an art that disrupts the official order of a censored yet unsilenced country. This essay seeks to bring from the confines of their restricted country women who, like Rosenfeld, defy authority each day, so they may reach us and tell us about themselves, their art and the forms in which they have survived and found a shared fulfillment. In addition to Rosenfeld, we will focus on the arpilleristas, women who create hauntingly beautiful tapestries from scraps of cloth, and two photographers: Paz Errázuriz and Roser Bru.

Women in Chile have not traditionally played a prominent role in the arts. Even today, most of the works exhibited in museums and galleries were created by men. However, the majority of the country's rural artisans have always been women. Today, women in the countryside still embroider lovely, elaborate tapestries, and create traditional clay casseroles and dishes. Yet, for the most part, women's handwork is not highly valued as a means of artistic expression, and women artisans are poorly paid.

The women artists introduced in this paper are making a strong impact on the Chilean art world while maintaining their ties to traditional women's art. Each group has taken an established medium — needlework, photography and drawing

— and has made it its own by adding certain innovative and subversive touches. As we will see, the political and social overtones of these works have had an important effect both within and beyond the Chilean art world.

Perhaps one of the most amazing phenomena of the Pinochet dictatorship, which has lasted almost thirteen years, is the fact that, in spite of the state of terror, *"Chile vive,"* Chile lives. Chile's streets and people, including their ways of speaking and their behaviour, are as lively as ever on the surface, masking the underlying terror. Where and how does one express oneself in a country that has been overwhelmed by fear? Where does one take refuge amidst the pain and despair? These are some of the questions that have been posed by artists, from popular artisans to those with works in the most exclusive galleries. Artists in both the cities and the countryside have begun to challenge the silence and defy the contemptible system that has been established by the military authority.

Many unofficial street performances have been achieved in Pinochet's Chile in which an individual places him / herself in the core of a city in crisis. In this way, the city's inhabitants become the central theme of the art. They become the objects and material of a creation that is vital and alive. From this are born what are called "art actions."

Among the actions that are now a part of the collective memory is one in which milk trucks blocked traffic and then drove with bottles of milk toward the neediest sectors of the city. The public observed the trucks, and immediately deciphered the subtle message behind the action: the truck drivers were defying the dictatorship by distributing milk to the poor. Similar art actions have occurred sporadically since 1981.

These first attempts at transforming the censured reality of the country stem from popular art, and are declarations of a silenced people who refuse to keep quiet. Another example of this process are the arpilleras of Chile, which are a reinterpretation of a folk tradition. They are spontaneous creations of art, born from the need to express the new metaphors operating in society, and whose cultural messages relate to the real, historical situation of the inhabitants.

Arpilleras are appliquéd wall hangings that are made from leftovers, unused objects, and pieces of thrown-out cloth. Beautiful, detailed tapestries, full of colour and sun, are constructed from things that have been discarded. The arpilleras project an image that is absolutely clear, and transmit specific messages such as "No More Torture," "Zone of Hunger" and "Zone of Pain."

The arpilleristas, the women who create arpilleras, began as a group in 1974, the year after the military dictatorship came to power. The Vicaria de la Solidaridad, a Catholic organization, sponsored workshops where women could go in the evenings to make arpilleras and earn money to help support their families. In many cases, the husbands of these women had been kidnapped and killed by the repressive government.

The messages transmitted by the arpilleras immediately capture the urgency of the women's situations. The women who make arpilleras are leading the way in challenging the system by using something purely traditional — needlework — as a weapon that defies silence and the imposed order. Because of the defiance of censorship and the subversive themes represented in the arpilleras, the arpilleristas must remain anonymous to protect both themselves and their families.

The arpillera also integrates itself into a very interesting phenomenon in Chile today: the utilization of one's own body in the creation of an artistic object or, better said, the creation of living art. Often, the women who make the arpilleras do not possess the necessary materials, so they fabricate art from their own bodies. For example, hair, fingernails and skirts become part of the textile on which they are working. In this way, the body and the created object are metaphors related to the essence of the creator, and are not acts distanced from the country's socio-historical reality.

In the areas of needlework and popular arts, daily scenes have become part of the artistic creation; in the field of photography, something similar has occurred. Perhaps in this area more than in any other, under authoritarianism, the artist has had to rethink the way in which photography can respond to a new social system that manipulates the country's entire reality. Two visual artists have been instrumental in this process: Paz Errázuriz and Roser Bru.

Paz Errázuriz is a young Chilean photographer who won a Guggenheim Fellowship in 1986. Errázuriz was born in Santiago, Chile in 1941. After working as an elementary school teacher, Errázuriz dedicated herself to photography in 1972. In 1973, she published a children's book, *Amalia*, for which she both wrote the text and provided photographs. Errázuriz has had exhibitions in Chile, France and Germany. Several of her photographs are in the permanent collection of the Fine Arts Museum of the University of Santiago, Chile. Errázuriz does not name her photographs; she believes the images speak for themselves.

Errázuriz's work is characterized by her focus on the marginal areas that the authoritarian government has tried to eradicate. For example, Errázuriz photographed prostitutes in hospitals on the verge of death. Beggars, people considered to be anomalies by a fascist society, unveil themselves before the spectator. The viewer, disarmed by the sharpness and clarity of the photographic image, now participates in an unseen, marginal world that makes itself visible.

There is a great respect and delicacy in the photographs of Paz Errázuriz in that the photographic negative does not manipulate or tamper with reality. Errázuriz lets the image float at random; for this reason, the subjects, like the beggars and the patients in the psychiatric hospital, are captured exactly as they are in their essence. Sometimes these people are blinded and are not able to see themselves as they truly are, because they are living under inhumane and deceitful conditions.

Marginality, in all of its turbulence, forms the nucleus of Paz Errázuriz's photographs. Poverty and hunger often appear as if these horrible metaphors of misery were part of the minutiae of everyday living. The characters that Errázuriz's camera selects are part of a circus of deaf people, one-eyed people and mutes. They embrace, wander and pass time in a country where treatment of life resembles a circus of death. Paradoxically, the mental patients, street-walkers and drug addicts go out into and live in the streets of Santiago. With their eccentricity, they occupy another space in the invisible sector of society, but they also exist in the visible and true reality of poverty, marginality and hunger. The disturbing space occupied by the milk trucks also forms part of the strategy and defiance of Paz Errázuriz. Evil is part of the world; we all know it exists, but we do not want to get near it. Paz Errázuriz is successful in that the viewer is unable to maintain distance from the image that she transmits. On the contrary, the spectator cannot remain indifferent. In this way, the anomaly and the forbidden are integrated into a fascist order that maintains itself by cleaning the walls of the city, watering flowers, and manipulating spaces for a semi-perfect peace. Faced with the images produced by Errázuriz, no Chilean can deny the existence of an oppressed and neglected sector of society.

Roser Bru was born in Barcelona, Spain in 1923. In 1939, she boarded a boat for Chile, now her second country. Bru has been a painter of international renown since 1973. Her works have been exhibited in Santiago, Barcelona, Madrid, Mexico, Buenos Aires and Berlin. Bru's photograph/paintings can be found in the permanent collections of the Metropolitan Museum in New York, the Museum of Modern Art of Rio de Janeiro, and the Museum of Modern Art of Santiago. The city of Barcelona recently published a catalogue of her work entitled, *Roser Bru: una mirada desde Fora* ("Roser Bru: A View from the Outside").

Like Errázuriz, Bru works with photography as a way to reclaim space taken and mutilated under authoritarianism. For Bru as well as for Errázuriz, photography is a record, a way to save and preserve, without intervention, daily events in the country. One of the techniques used by both artists is the superimposition of different fragments of reality. For example, in one of Bru's works, we see newspaper clippings that speak of the prosperity of the nation juxtaposed with a photograph of a small, undernourished girl with flaccid breasts prostituting herself for a crust of bread.

The fragmented, discontinuous and sketched reality assumes, then, a singular importance within the visual and graphic scope utilized by Chilean artists. In the same way, the use of video as a means of documentation has increased in the years of authoritarianism, and filming during demonstrations has been used constantly.

One of Roser Bru's most striking works, which has reached the cities as well as various international centres, is the photographic collage entitled "Lila Valderrama." Bru uses a painting of Lila's face as a background, depicting her with her eyes blindfolded and bloody. On the side of the portrait is a license photograph with Valderrama's identification number and an inscription that says: "Disappeared." The photograph testifies that this face exists. In seeing it, we are forced to practice the art of remembrance.

In a single artist, Lotti Rosenfeld represents the diverse ways in which art actions in Chile since 1973, particularly actions accomplished by women, have begun to form a legacy or tradition of opposition to authoritarianism and its manifestations. Her physical presence, kneeling and drawing lines on the pavement from the White House in Washington, D.C., to the Andean mountains between Argentina and Chile, to the barracks of General Pinochet, is a form of defiance and interruption of order. Rosenfeld not only disrupts the flow of traffic, but rebels against everything the authoritarian government represents. She uses systems of destruction and deconstruction to sketch out, for example, vertical lines instead of horizontal ones on traffic signs. In this way, the artist commands instant attention from the passersby and the automobile drivers. By altering street signs, she creates an optical illusion that leads to a questioning of all prevailing codes of communication.

In an interview in Santiago in 1986, Lotti Rosenfeld summarized the motivations behind her art: "To alter a symbol that regulates transit is to demonstrate the symbol's international significance, and to reveal the daily forms of power where it operates in terms of the imposition of order. Also, to make crosses on the pavement is to disrupt our routine submission to symbols, and to create an appreciation for the symbolism in our surroundings."

From the women who make arpilleras to record, save and help their loved ones to the photographs of Paz Errázuriz and Roser Bru that search for and reveal hidden structures and the stories of the invisible members of society, we observe women who, in times of profound social, economic and historical crisis, transform their realities by means of an artistic object. They do not intend to obscure the reality in which they find themselves. On the contrary, they intend to restore reality and show it to the spectator. By making visible Chile's current reality, they defy the power of the oppressors.

We have noted how women artists have found a way to express themselves in repressive Chile. Women have left their homes and the private sphere to participate in the public, political life of their country. Their forms of expression — needlework, photography and drawing — have become true channels of political and artistic expression. With the exception of the arpilleristas, these artists were born into a privileged position, but have managed to give a voice to those who had been silenced by repression and poverty. The women cited in these pages confirm that, in times of historical turmoil, art redeems and transforms a society that has been mutilated by injustice and pain to make it fully human and sane.

BIBLIOGRAPHY

For other studies related to popular art in countries of political turmoil and historical dislocation, see Guy Brett, *Through Our Own Eyes*, New Society Publishing, 1968. This book contains a chapter on the Chilean arpilleras. For a detailed study of the visual arts in Chile since 1973, see "Margins and Institutions: Art in Chile since 1973" by Nelly Richards in a special issue of *Art and Text* (Sidney, Australia). Also see Lucy Lippard, *Get the Message*.

Ceremonies of a Sliced Body: Frida Kahlo

More than any other Latin American woman artist, Frida Kahlo invented herself in a dignified, ceremonious fashion, searching for the gestures, colours and costumes of life and death. Her self-portraits are the story of a sliced life, the fate of a broken body brought to painting with a realism and originality unequalled in Hispanic American art.

In this essay, I will not talk about Frida's life with details and recollections of her anxious moments, but rather will attempt to emphasize the significant elements in the development of this Latin American artist who created a universe composed of her own, broken body. No other woman painter or poet has spoken so profoundly and accurately about the female body as Frida Kahlo. Her paintings are narratives, celebrations of births, miscarriages and funerals, and her art is linked to the fears and secrets of women, companions of birth and death.

Each of Frida's self-portraits contains a mask, whether it be that of Tehuana, of the woman entwined in the roots of the earth, of life or of the omens of death. The mask becomes a face and the face becomes a credible image for those who contemplate it. In Frida's life, the act of painting converts common elements into transcendental themes. Thus, a basket full of flowers or Frida's hands covered with rings become a way to survive solitude and deny death.

In Frida's self-portraits, many of her expressions, her looks that pierce the spectator, are dramatized by certain brush strokes; for example, the connection of her eyebrows. These gestures demonstrate that Frida Kahlo paints, lives and survives in the presence of pain. To survive the illnesses and long hospital visits, Frida dressed in scarves and winged skirts that seemed to fly despite her missing leg and broken spine. Her body, plundered and pierced, becomes the most memorable element of her paintings.

Few women have portrayed themselves with Frida's hallu-
cinatory honesty. In numerous self-portraits, she appears to be
telling a story: solitary, bleak plains, infertile lives, and an open
and split body. The image of Frida linked to a solitary landscape,
to a vast, immobile sky, is constantly reiterated.

The body of the woman, affected, aching, broken and
cruelly exposed to the vicissitudes of life or fate was delineated
by Kahlo in a form that was unique. This is particularly true of
Kahlo's works from the 1930s, when she and Diego Rivera found
themselves in Detroit. In the painting, *Henry Ford Hospital*,
Kahlo depicts a miscarriage. Frida appears in a pool of blood,
the white sheet contrasting the death of the fetus and a womb
swollen with a pregnancy that no longer exists. Here, we see the
image of a woman's open body relating to herself, keeping watch
over herself, shaped by the metaphor of her own being. Floating
objects also appear, including an orchid and a small fetus that
looks like Diego Rivera, all symbols of a truncated motherhood.

In *Nacimiento* ("Birth"), Frida appears giving birth to
herself, but what is born is a dead infant. Few women have
portrayed themselves and that which is born and dies within one's
own body with such startling realism. Kahlo incorporated the
tradition of the peasant women who are involved with the
ceremonies of life and the shrouds of death on a daily basis. This
realism leaves the spectator perplexed and dazzled because, how
often does a woman paint herself giving birth to death? Within
Frida's narrative portraits also appear certain zones dark with
her own, unique symbolism and an agglomeration of floating
objects.

We could refer to these zones as zones of pain, where
memory participates with the fragments to create a deeper level
of symbolism. Kahlo, in composing the story of her sliced and
broken body, presents the fantasies of everything possible but
not realized, now transformed by the pain of loss and absence.
More than depicting the anguish of a woman who lacks a round
nest to reproduce herself, Frida Kahlo painted and exorcised
herself. By sketching and inventing herself, she recreated with

great honesty her own absences, the absences of lost children and the absences of Diego Rivera caused by his indifference and his interest in other women.

It is almost impossible to forget the painting, *Las dos Fridas* ("Two Fridas"), where two bodies are united by blood, those threads of blood that comprise a constant allusion to a ruined life. Frida painted *Las dos Fridas* when she was separated from Diego Rivera for the first time. More than the pain or rupture of separation, *Las dos Fridas* is a representation of the dual identity that was so prevalent in Frida's works: that is to say, Frida on the threshold of life and death, Frida divided and flagellated. The essence of a body that suffers and cries can be found in the contrasting masks that the artist creates.

In *Las dos Fridas*, the white light that emanates from the clothing of one Frida contrasts with the other Frida, darker, dressed in a typical peasant outfit. This dichotomy creates the illusion that Frida's body is divided into fragments of light and dark. The dual configuration of light and shadow, also represented in the body that simultaneously provides birth and death, encompasses Kahlo's fantasies.

In this context, the term fantasy has nothing to do with the inherent surrealism of the period, nor with Breton's classifications. Frida did not create her images through a subconscious necessity for invention. Instead, she transformed her painful reality into a ceremonious fantasy that began with the incorporation of her own clothing as an instrument of magic and beliefs.

Mexico, with its incalculable popular riches, marvellous votive art and frenetic cult of death and life, became a special aspect of Kahlo's painting, as, for example, in the work, *Mi nana y yo* ("My nurse and I"). Frida's self-portrait appears again, suckling from her wet nurse: an Indian woman representing the affirmation of Mexican culture with its ancestral roots, its alchemy and its cult of fertility. The plants, sky and magic of abundance represent indigenous Mexico, because the woman's milk seems to be part of the sky from which it emanates. *Niña con la máscara* ("Girl with the Mask") is another instance of the preoccupation with and incorporation of an autochthonous Mexican culture. In this painting, a small child who looks like Frida appears carrying a zempazuchil, the Aztec flower of death.

Kahlo's adoption of primitivism in her painting from the 1940s to the end of her life was previously reflected in certain elements of her work but, in particular, in her careful selection of her clothing. Frida's style, her scarves, the rings on each finger and the constant presence of death influenced her self-portraits and her charm. Kahlo gave birth to herself and created herself; in this way, she produced an image of herself that incorporated the grandeur of Mexican art and the adoption of a popular style.

Frida's primitivism, with its drama and a certain naiveté, forms a pictorial universe that lends itself to the game of life and death as well as to the masking and unmasking of pain and happiness. Also, the still lifes that Frida painted are associated with her fervent emphasis on "Mexican-ness." She does not depict ordinary fruit, but prickly pears and watermelons, fruit with a sexual dimension surrounded by an arid and desolate landscape. The painting, *Frutas de la tierra* ("Fruits of the Earth"), alludes to the stages of life, including birth, life and death. However, the obvious imperfection of the fruit suggests that life has been difficult for these objects and their survival has stemmed from a profound desire to live. Frida continually appropriated objects and converted them into symbols of her obsessions, paintings and experiences.

Kahlo's last exhibition took place in 1953, a year before her death. Kahlo attended this exhibition on a stretcher. Her biographers recount that almost all of the Mexican intelligentsia attended this retrospective, as well as a group of handicapped people. The event reflected Frida's characteristic drama, and she again reaffirmed her love of life, denying and defying death in her final months.

When Kahlo died, her body was cremated. It is said that, as her body entered the oven, her intense, dark hair shone full of life's fire because Frida Kahlo had not died. Her self-portraits accompany us in our lonely hours and gravitate in our memories like a chiaroscuro that passes between the zones of light and darkness.

Frida Kahlo painted herself but she also unveiled the stories of women who give birth to pools of blood, who miscarry. She knew how to capture our intrinsic duality, because *Las dos Fridas* is the story of women between vigils and dreams, of those who, full of uncertainties, dare to know themselves, paint themselves and create themselves.

Kahlo, marked by the traces of pain from her early adolescence, dominated by a perpetually open wound, full of signs and threats, learned how to survive through colour and the creation of an artistic space full of the living and the dead. Death was never a secret for Frida, because it always surrounded her. Even in her still lifes, pieces of fruit become strange figures that wander through zones of the inexpressible and the unexplainable.

Thanks to her insatiable and obstinate will, Frida Kahlo surpassed her wounds. She plotted her destiny through her painting, and never exhausted her desire to explore the riches within herself. For this reason, repetition is almost non-existent in Kahlo's self-portraits. In each brush stroke, new gestures and scraps of life appear.

Perhaps no other Latin American artist knew how to create through the reconstruction of a broken body: broken in her legs, broken in her spinal column and, more than anything, broken in her fertility. Kahlo's pictorial contribution not only resides in her majestic technique and balance of colours and forms, but also in the narratives of her life that reflect the history of women. Finally, she dared to speak with an unequalled clarity about miscarriages, fetuses and unconsumed lives. Frida Kahlo gives us life, because she was born dying and created dying. She created a mode of painting that, by focussing on the artist herself, teaches us to examine ourselves.

For more information on Frida Kahlo, see the following biographies:

Frida *by Hayden Herrera, Harper & Row, 1983.*

El Pincel de la Angustia *by Marta Zamora, Edición a Cargo de Zamora, Mexico City, 1987.*

Roser Bru or The Vigilant Memory

Memory, exile and nostalgia characterize the pictorial trajectory of Roser Bru. Born in Barcelona in 1923, where she completed her first years of university study, Bru left the country by ship in 1939 for distant Chile, now her second country. The memory of the Spanish Civil War and the advent of the Second World War on the same day that this adolescent arrived at the port of Valparaíso were the coordinates that later delineated her work.

Another key event in Bru's life was the Chilean military coup of 1973, which also left a deep scar on her work. The coup became interlaced with her memories of the Spanish Civil War, the concentration camps and the disappeared. Roser incorporated all of these elements into her painting and writing for, as she has stated, her work is her text.

In a recent retrospective catalogue published by Barcelona's municipal government covering almost a decade of Bru's unique photograph/paintings, the artist said the following: "Death and memory are preoccupations that become obsessions in my works of art" from 1973 on. And it is precisely this aspect of memory that is developed and revealed through the woodcut prints she interposes with photographs, converting them into attractive yet threatening elements. Thus, in Bru's work, memory forms a repeating textile-texture-text that began to develop in the 1970s and that the artist herself consciously incorporates.

There are certain sequences of images that make an impression on the observer, since they reveal the history or memory of dead individuals who return to look at us, to denounce us in our survival. For example, the faces of Franz Kafka and his lover, Milena Jesenska Pollak, appear together, inert and almost identical, linked by a predestined fate.

Kafka and Milena appear to be the observers of a history that left them mute, silenced, but always united by destiny. These two historical characters also form an intra-history in that the person who looks at these photographs is impregnated with pain and memory. In this way, the observer transcends the photographs to become a witness to Kafka and Milena's story, to become a survivor. Through the photographs that Bru selects, she weaves together relationships. She establishes innumerable links embedded in a collective memory. The decomposition, the occasional absence of colour and the lines that scratch out, underline and erase but always unite, are the elements of these texts of absence where the image of forgetfulness is carefully mixed with the image of remembrance.

Through photography, missing objects are recovered, and a little of life is redeemed from death. The photographs of Kafka-Milena mentioned above, and one depicting the death of a Spanish Republican taken by Robert Capa begin to give a concrete form to the texts, to the images through the embodiment of funerary rites. The photograph/paintings do not only allude to a historical figure but, through the precision of the friendly bonds that are forged in her works, Bru is also able to incorporate each individual into the human family.

Here, it is fitting to mention Roser Bru's interest in incorporating written texts in her works, and in their relationship with the pictorial images. Various examples of this combination exist in the series dedicated to Gabriela Mistral. In these works, we notice Mistral's watchful look which appears to observe us, and her accusatory expression that is between pious and diabolical.

Gabriela also appears in works as an adolescent and as a school teacher who is canonized and later erased, bound by a rigid code that does not permit her to be herself. In one work, there appear two images of Gabriela's face, this time not taken from photographs but instead, from Bru's memory that invents and creates. The faces are united, in the same way that Kafka and Milena's images were linked. A denunciatory Gabriela accuses us with a look that says, Why did they canonize me? Why didn't they just let me be myself? In this work, Mistral appears with the dates of her birth and death. Her face is outlined in violet and red, colours that sweetly mark her accusing face. The details are presented so we do not forget her.

A similar technique is utilized in the photograph/painting of a disappeared woman, Lila Valdenegro. It is a painting framed by a photograph from an identification card. The disappeared woman possesses a look that questions and begs, but that also vanishes behind a gas or reddish veil that mists or covers her eyes. The search for these faces is Roser Bru's legacy. She searched for the Gabriela Mistral who was sanctified by others in the same way that she looked for the face of Lila Valdenegro.

The disappeared woman looks at us as if, through her gaze, the observer could find her and bring her back. Her look possesses a sinister ambivalence that is both lyrical and otherworldly, accusatory not only toward the torturer who binds her but also toward the observer. It is impossible to forget the disappeared woman with I.D. number 353 located within a frame, within a painting, within a text. The work is an indication that the woman is present and that she exists, which produces a contradiction since she is missing.

Women's bodies, together with their belongings, their surroundings and their changeable corporality, form another component of Roser Bru's work. Bru uses the image-metaphor of the watermelon to elaborate the vital, feminine concept of the body that gives life and death. The watermelon represents a plenitude of colour, a harmonic roundness but also, the watermelon is a rupture, an error or disillusion.

This perspective can be seen in Bru's portraits of Frida Kahlo. Here, Bru recreates Kahlo's desired but fruitless maternity through the image of a watermelon. The watermelon is broken and slips away from Kahlo's disfigured body like threads or flames of blood. Bru also uses the watermelon as a metaphor for Violeta Parra, who gave life through her songs but who also caused her own death.

Roser Bru represents a vigilent memory because images, icons, rituals and funeral elements are united in a collective past. Ann Frank is the innocent Ann of the concentration camps who is similar to Lila Valdenegro. When we look at her, we are like her, like all of them because their memory is no longer alien to us, it is ours to judge, keep or reject.

Eyes take on a particular colour in Bru's sorrowful photograph/paintings. At times, the eyes seem to be covered by gray clouds that separate them from the observer. In other instances, the eyes are tinted with light tones of purple and red, and accented with huge drops of blood that seem to have fallen from the paint brush. Bru's work is also characterized by her sketches and her short and unorganized brush strokes. These elements are signs, traces and clues for following the footsteps of her pictorial-memorial work, work that attempts, not to defeat oblivion, only to be and to remember.

Roser Bru is one of the most outstanding painters in Latin American and Catalonia. Her photograph/paintings have been shown in numerous personal exhibitions in Santiago, Barcelona, Ibiza, Madrid, Mexico, Buenos Aires and Berlin. Her works can be found in the permanent collections of various museums, including the Metropolitan Museum of Art in New York, and the Museums of Modern Art in Rio de Janeiro and Santiago. Recently, the city of Barcelona dedicated a retrospective of her work, with a catalogue entitled: *Roser Bru: Una Mirada desde Fora* ("Roser Bru: A Look from the Outside"). Bru currently lives in Santiago and travels frequently to Barcelona.

Metaphors of
Female Political Ideology:
The Cases of Chile and Argentina[1]

During the 1970s, Latin America was dominated by repressive, military governments that tortured and kidnapped individuals, and attempted to maintain their power indefinitely. Ten years later, the authoritarian governments of Latin America are the exception, with only two remaining in power: the regimes of Stroessner in Paraguay and of Pinochet in Chile.

In most countries under dictatorial regimes, women have participated in the fight against the politics of terror from a new and different perspective, developing metaphors and symbols that have already come to form part of a collective female political ideology. The purpose of this essay is to examine some of the ways in which women have become involved in politics in two countries of the Southern Cone, Chile and Argentina. I intend to demonstrate that there exists a uniquely female political ideology, as shown by the metaphoric and symbolic content of the protests against violence.

Historically, the movement of the Mothers of the Plaza de Mayo constituted the first political response to the disappearance of Argentine citizens, a policy implemented by the military government in March of 1976.[2] The group originated in a modest fashion, starting with fourteen women who met each other through the long, formal procedures and pilgrimages in search of their missing loved ones. From this, the movement was born, motivated by a concrete circumstance: the loss of loved ones. Partisan ideology was not an issue for this group of women; they were motivated by a common pain. From its birth, this group stimulated the social movement towards the transition to democracy in Argentina. These women were the only ones to publicly protest the repression in Argentina. Later, they would be followed by other women in Chile, El Salvador, Guatemala and Uruguay.[3]

The metaphor of the plaza and the silent and solitary march was converted into an essential symbolic aspect of the fight of these women. They chose a place where women had traditionally been prohibited from gathering: the plaza. Within Argentine society, the plaza is a public space dominated by patriarchy, just as all of the buildings that surround the plaza, the banks, businesses and government offices, are dominated by that same masculine power. The women added their presence to this male domain, leaving their private and traditional settings, their homes, and their daily battle for bread to feed their families.

The women united in a collective action of solidarity that sprang from their biological roles as mothers. It is precisely this role that made them develop a uniquely female set of images within the political sphere. The mothers constituted a group of women that, without worrying about the ideology of changing their sex roles, produced an enormous change in the female consciousness.[4] The collective nature of the protest challenged the stereotype that characterizes women as not being able to organize. It also demonstrated that the resignation, weakness and passivity considered to be typical female characteristics are also false.

The white kerchiefs worn by the Mothers of the Plaza de Mayo came to be recognized by the entire world as an example of the metaphors of female political symbology. The white kerchief is a symbol of women in the collective memory of many societies. The kerchief is knotted, implying the lack of freedom. The fact that the hair remains covered is a symbol of repression within the ideology of women. Within the rhetoric of dress, the kerchief represents the female role. Nevertheless, the kerchief worn by the Mothers of the Plaza de Mayo has been changed, revised and elaborated under a new canon: the kerchief is embroidered with the name of the child who has disappeared.

The kerchief is an object that covers the hair, keeping it invisible. When the name of a lost child is embroidered onto the kerchief, that name becomes visible, and gives a new symbolic meaning to the kerchief. The fact that the child's name is embroidered by hand reflects the connection between the hand that creates the name and the bearer of that name. That is to say, the two bodies, the one identified on the head of the woman and the woman herself, are united.

The embroidered name has a more profound significance within the female symbology. Throughout history, women have been characterized by the activity of embroidering. For women, sewing has been a form of writing a text. To link sewing with the kerchief is a way to expose this text; when exhibited on a woman's head, it becomes a metaphor of the private and public.

For the Mothers of the Plaza de Mayo, the symbol of the white kerchief has the following connotation: "We began using this colour because it is the symbol of peace, something that unites us with all mothers."[5] Also, when referring to their belief in non-violence and to their marches, they point out the following:

> *We tried not to be aggressive with words, thinking that our children were hostages. Non-violence was also a way of defending ourselves; we knew that if we created violence, it could generate a reaction that was contrary to what we were trying to achieve.*[6]

The white kerchiefs and the slow, silent, circular march around the pyramid in the Plaza de Mayo create a female political character. The silence reflects the silence imposed on the female gender for centuries, which relegated women to waiting, to resignation. But here, silence holds a new significance. It is a silence that accuses, a silence that asks, "Where are our children?"

The activity that takes place every Thursday in the Plaza de Mayo was born from a break with the dominant ideology. Here, there are no slogans or pamphlets. The action is separate from all partisan activities and separates itself from the male political ideology. The mothers define themselves as defenders of life, and as a movement that is not passive, but pacifist. This is crucial for understanding female political activity under authoritarian governments, where death becomes a gratuitous instrument of the torturer. In societies ruled by dictatorships, the ideology of death is the prevailing force that dominates and contrasts with the ideology of life and, above all, with the right to protect life.

In addition, the symbology of photography has also been an important instrument in the female protest movements. Photographs are associated with the metaphor of embroidering the name on the kerchief, that is to say, with memory and remembering. The Mothers of the Plaza de Mayo and, later, members of other movements in Latin America such as the Group of Mutual Support formed in Guatemala in 1983, and the Association of the Detained and Disappeared formed in Chile in 1979, carry photographs of their missing relatives during the protests.

The symbolism of the photograph rises to various levels. In the first place, the photograph is tied to the chest of the person who carries it, emphasizing the link between the body of the living person and the search for the missing individual or dead body. Also, it produces a strong visual image. The photograph is tied to a woman who in reality is saying, *"This face is mine, it is part of my body and I have the right to find it."*

As a metaphorical symbol, the photograph gives the person who carries it the image of a past, as Susan Sontag explains in her book, *Oh Photography.*[7] The past is always somewhat unreal, especially in the case of the disappeared because no one knows where they are and there are no tombs or altars to visit. The photograph gives effective possession of that which seems unreal, since the disappearance of these people took place as if by a diabolical magic act. Also, the photograph of the missing person carried around the neck or on the chest of a woman gives an obsessive and uniquely cohesive image on which to focus.

The individual who observes this face and knows the historical context of the protest begins to worry, to the point of becoming obsessed with knowing more about the private and political history of the individual. The face that is carried on the woman's chest belongs to a living, immediate history. The loss does not only appear in books, but is profoundly present, and is tied to a woman, evidence of its existence.

The action in the Plaza, the silent march, the white kerchiefs with the embroidered names and the photographs that stare out at the passersby emphasize the symbolic, metaphoric act of the Mothers of the Plaza de Mayo. This semiotic of dress reflects non-violence and peacefulness as well as public suffering. The persistence of these rituals of continual protest, which have taken place since 1977, helps to create a powerful image of repetition and familiarity. Now the general public, from the generals who observe these women from their balconies to the passersby, becomes part of this collective vigil. The pain becomes public.

The strategies *and rules for carrying out political action observed in the Mothers of the Plaza de Mayo, motivated by a moral, but not moralizing doctrine, are also utilized by the women of Chile today. The techniques they use include the appeal to other groups within the country and the communal search for truth and justice. It is very possible that the Mothers of the Plaza de Mayo have influenced their Chilean compañeras. Perhaps the future will show profound connections between these movements of female resistance.

In 1983, a critical year for political activity against Pinochet's government, women were an essential element of protest and were visible in the fight against authoritarianism. In Chile that year, a unique movement was formed called "Women for Life."[8] The name gives an indication of the nature of the movement, showing a clear parallel to the movement of the Mothers of the Plaza de Mayo whose slogan is "In search of life; we want them to be alive."

Unlike the movements in Argentina, El Salvador and Guatemala, Women for Life is not exclusively a movement of mothers, but rather a collective initially formed by twenty-six women of different political leanings and social classes. These women resolved to fight against repression, torture and fear through a general appeal that called all Chilean women to join in the struggle against the dictatorship. In a theatre in Santiago, "El Caupolicán," ten-thousand women of all social and economic classes met. The theme of the meeting was "Freedom's Name is Woman." This meeting was so successful and emotional that the movement continues to work secretly.

The structure of Women for Life and its strategies for carrying out political tasks are clearly different from the techniques employed by men. The members of Women for Life, like the Mothers of the Plaza de Mayo, are not motivated or directed by political parties. Obviously, individual members belong to different parties, but they are all motivated by a common belief in the power of dialogue. They practice democratic political encounters in an open fashion. That is to say, the collective, Women for Life, has been able to draw from other movements of women throughout the country, such as the movement of working-class women and the feminist movement. It is through this dialogue that ideological differences are resolved and non-violent protest and solidarity are practiced.

Women for Life is an example of a movement that operates based on a series of symbolic gestures and actions. For example, at times, groups of women march in the plazas of Santiago, carrying photographs of the missing and detained, invoking their names, demonstrating that their loved ones are present and alive through their voices and memories.

The insistence that this movement is "for life" creates an ideology tied to rebirth and hope. The emphasis on life contrasts with the death to which the country submits on a daily basis. The rituals of collective marches, support for human rights organizations, fasts for political prisoners, and protests on International Women's Day can be attributed to the constant labour and shared participation of Women for Life with other groups working for social and political reform within the country.

Among the actions of public protest carried out by Women for Life are the peaceful marches in central parts of the city. The marches usually begin in three different places. The women carry coloured ribbons and join the ribbons together in one spot. Some of the slogans used in these demonstrations are: "Freedom's Name is Woman," "Let's go, woman," "No more because we are more," and the most recent, "1986 is ours. Women's Word."

The group, Women for Life, has performed many, varied activities in its short life and has implemented vast changes in a society dominated by patriarchy and violence. The most prominent metaphors of this movement allude to the visibility of women in public areas of the city: in plazas, gardens, and in the different sectors, including the popular sectors and upper-class neighbourhoods. One of the group's most important contributions has been the implementation of non-violent strategies throughout a city and country that are dominated by violence.

Photographs also occupy a fundamental place in the set of symbols created by Women for Life. In addition to attempting to save their loved ones from oblivion, Women for Life uses the photographs to appeal to a moral, collective consciousness that embraces the entire country. The organization put up posters throughout the country, particularly in Santiago, of Loreta Castillo, a young student who was tortured in August, 1984. After torturing her, the secret police dynamited her body and publicly denounced her as being a terrorist. The photograph of Loreta Castillo acts as a reminder of this tragedy. She appears smiling, full of life, and rejecting death.

The occupation of various public spaces and the covering of walls with the faces of the victims of the dictatorship are part of the metaphorization and daily activity of these women in cities oppressed by dictatorship, hatred, and continual hunger. Women for Life's activities are always open and visible. In general, the protests are carried out during the day and in clearly visible spaces, reinforcing the fact that these women do not have anything to hide, as opposed to the torture, disappearances and clandestine prisons that are hidden in Chile by the government.

The women wear their hair out, loose, and they wear light-coloured clothing. Their steps defy fear, and their hands are always open to reflect another of their slogans, "We Have Clean

Hands." Their hands have never burned or tortured anyone. This metaphorical ritual of openness contrasts with the police in Chile, who wander through the streets after sunset with their faces painted black and their uniforms full of weapons. The woman project an image of life, opposing the image of death projected by the police.

Among Women for Life's common strategies for carrying out political action are constant attempts to initiate dialogue with the opposition. Overcoming their fear, the women pass out pamphlets to educate members of the opposition. Other techniques are direct observation of the police and face-to-face confrontation. In this way, the women defeat terror. During the marches, we observe the participants as they attempt to speak with the police who line the streets, preventing the columns of women from moving on.[9] Posters that read "We Are More" and "Soldier, Chile Needs You" are ways of saying, "We are here, meet us face to face." This tactic is typical of non-violent movements, and accentuates Women for Life's desire for solidarity and collective mobilization in Chile.[10]

On Wednesday, October 30, 1985, Women for Life sponsored a general march of approximately five-thousand women. The following statement was read aloud: "We are more for justice, we are more for democracy, we are more for solidarity, we are more for life, we are more." For Women for Life, there are no more partisan ideologies but instead, a globalization of the collective desires of women who are dominated by the wish for the restoration of a free, just and dignified country.

The cases of the Mothers of the Plaza de Mayo and Women for Life are examples of political movements formed by women that continue to grow and develop. They are primarily movements that were born from practice and through practice, not theory. Both the Mothers of the Plaza de Mayo and Women for Life arose in response to a drastic necessity that affected women of every social class. The disappearance of loved ones and social injustice, especially hunger, forced women to unite and organize.

In response to authoritarianism, the private becomes public. Food and the lack of food become social and political issues of fundamental importance. The women, conscious of their role as providers of basic necessities and as guardians of the family, organize themselves around these domestic issues and fight. In the case of the Mothers of the Plaza de Mayo, contact with jails was of fundamental importance in motivating the women. In the case of Women for Life, everything began with a group of friends who saw the need to present an alternative to fascism. They resorted to grouping women in different communal kitchens, and in this way, groups of women were born, formed from the politics of necessity and in search of a public voice.

Politics and rebellion were born from daily experience. These movements of women still do not concern themselves with hierarchies, power and order, but rather function more from similarities than from differences. The attitudes of solidarity, togetherness, and democratic decision-making are the parameters of these two groups that are attempting to create a system of harmony and peace in order to fight against the dominant systems of violence and repression.

The negation of authoritarianism and the establishment of democracy in the country as well as in the home are the goals of female political activity in these two countries of the Southern Cone. These manifestations of non-violence have, or are beginning to have, great repercussions. We can see how the Mothers of the Plaza de Mayo was at first a movement exclusively of the mothers of individuals who had disappeared. Now, the organization has begun to include other groups, not only of mothers but of all citizens interested in human rights and the freedom of human beings. The same happened with Women for Life, which has been able to convene all sectors of Chilean society more successfully than the opposition groups that are dominated by men.

The institutionalized hierarchy of political values has disappeared in the two movements cited. The central concerns of these women are the right to life and the right to exist in peace in a patriarchal culture where death and fear are daily strategies used by the government to terrorize the public.

The women, motivated by subsistence needs, and by wishes of unity and of achieving common good, are the ones who fight in favour of life. One of Women for Life's press releases stated: "The women sleep each night in fear that our neighbourhood or our house might be destroyed, or that one of us might be kidnapped or disappear forever. In the face of so much destruction, horror and hunger the women cannot, do not want, as workers and as neighbours, to continue to wait. We demand that our public officials accept their historic responsibility to lead the Chilean nation to liberation."[11]

The politicization of these groups of women does not follow established theories concerning collective mobilization. In the first place, these women made their original decision to go out in search of the truth without the intervention of political parties or male leaders. For this reason, the mothers' actions force a re-examination of preconceived theories about social movements, where women's movements are always considered to be passive and irrelevant to the general political situation. In the cases examined in this article, the opposite is shown. The division between the personal and the political disappears, especially in the case of the Mothers of the Plaza de Mayo. The mothers are the only ones who publicly protested the Falkland War; for this reason, the Mothers are an important force in the restoration or, better said, the maintenance of democracy at an ethical and ideological level in Argentina today.

In Chile, the women's protests against the military dictatorship have given a new air of legitimacy to women's movements. Notwithstanding the Chilean suffragists of the 1930s and 1940s who fought to secure women's right to vote, women always worked for and through political parties. Beginning in 1983, Chilean women proposed an answer to authoritarianism that came from within. One of the essential contributions of Women for Life has been the affirmation and establishment of feminism as a pacifist movement in complete opposition to the ruling authoritarianism.[12] Another contribution has been the negation of violence in public and official spaces and within the home. One of the slogans utilized in the protests is "Democracy in the country and in the home."

Conclusion

As described above, the Mothers of the Plaza de Mayo and Women for Life have developed a new form of political action from a perspective that is different from the traditional male perspective. These two groups have created a form of politics that is motivated by morality, the family and peace. However, I insist that these moral feelings are derived from a unique point of view and reflect a specific context. Morality implies defying death, and saying a loud "No" to any form of violence. For this reason, political action within the ideological context of these women's movements is motivated by a strong adherence to special codes, metaphors and symbols.

These women, both the Argentineans and the Chileans, support various types of movements, such as fasts, protests against torture, and defense for those who return from exile. That is to say, the political activities of these groups are carried out in ways that preserve the values of justice and, more than anything, humanity in the widest meaning of the term.

The fact that the Mothers of the Plaza de Mayo and Women for Life act as movements of transition towards democracy, and that they possess the power of collective mobilization and convocation reminds us that the massive demonstrations that have been initiated by these groups of women have given them a platform and political legitimacy. These groups have also been able to develop a new female political ideology and, above all, a new form of practicing democracy.

The white kerchiefs, the photographs tied to the body, the silent vigils, and the marchers with hands held high have already come to form part of women's collective imagery. Women carry out political activity in a different manner because they are different and their triumphs have begun to be different.

FOOTNOTES

1 Due to the limited amount of space, this work will focus on only two movements: the Mothers of the Plaza de Mayo in Argentina and Women for Life in Chile. Nevertheless, this set of political ideas and images exists in other countries as well, especially in Guatemala with the Group of Mutual Support. See, for example, *Guatemala: The Group of Mutual Support*, an America's Watch report, 1985.

2 See Elizabeth Jelin, *Los nuevos movimientos sociales*, Centro Editor de América Latina, p. 48.

   For more general information about the Mothers of the Plaza de Mayo, see:

   Jean Pierre Bousquet, *Las locas de la Plaza de Mayo*, Buenos Aires: El Cid, 1982.

   John Simpson and Jana Bennet, *The Disappeared and the Mothers of the Plaza*, New York: St. Martin's Press, 1985.

3 The literature that treats the theme of the transition to democracy is varied, although very little has been written about the fundamental role of women in this process. Among the most important are:

   Guillermo O'Donnell, *Transition from Authoritarian Rule*, Baltimore: Johns Hopkins University Press, 1986.

   Transición a la democracia en América Latina, edited by Francisco Orrego Vicuña, Buenos Aires: Grupo Editor Latinoamericano, 1985.

4 Temma has a very interesting article about the phenomenon of women's collective action in periods of crisis. See: "Female Consciousness and Collective Action: The Barcelona Casa 1910-1918," *Signs* 7, No. 3 (1982): 545-556.

5 Testimony of a mother. See Jelin, *Los nuevos movimientos*, p. 50.

6 Ibid.

7 Susan Sontag, *On Photography*, New York: Farrar, Strauss and Giroux, 1979.

8 Until now there has been only one unedited document circulated about Women for Life, compiled by Teresa Valdés. For a copy, write to Flacso, Leopoldo Urrutia 1950, Santiago, Chile.

9 This information about tactics useful to dominate fear appears in pamphlets that circulated throughout the city. Also, one of the most interesting books on the political thought of Chilean women from its origins is Julieta Kirkwood, *Las feministas y los partidos*, Santiago de Chile: Flacso, 1984.

10 To study the theory of non-violence, see Gene Sharp, *Social Power and Political Freedom*, Boston: Porter Sargent Publishers, 1980.

11 Press release, August 10, 1985.

12 For a basic bibliography on women and non-violence, see: *Piecing it Together: Feminism and Non-Violence* published by the Feminism and Non-Violence Study Group, 2 College Close, Buchleigh Westward Devon, 1983.

   Alison M. Jaggar, *Feminist Politics and Human Nature*, Totowa, New Jersey: Rowman and Allan Ltd., Publishers, 1983.

   Pam McAllister, *Reweaving the Web of Life*, New York: New Society Publishers, 1982.

The Word that is Heard:
The Testimony of Rigoberta Menchú

To confess, to return to the period of Scheherezade, to narrate and dare to speak in order to survive have become important objectives of Latin American narrative, especially that written by women. In the novels of yesteryear, the confession and the revelation of one's private life alluded exclusively to the internal dilemma of women who, despite the limitations of the period, took up the pen and wrote. Two well-known examples of this type of novel are *Ifigenia* (1922) by Teresa de la Parra, the confessional novel of a young, aristocratic Venezuelan woman, and *La última niebla* (1931) by María Luisa Bombal, the fictional reflection of a rich woman of the Chilean aristocracy immersed in the boredom of a bourgeois marriage.

All of the novels of this genre confess, recount and enunciate an intimate "I" with whom the reader can empathize. The act of confession in these works involves the discovery and uncovering of superficial elements, including the attire, environment and historical circumstances of the period.

It has been said that women confess their secrets through letters, diaries and secret papers because their access to public confession has been impeded. The great exploits, novels of adventure, and confessions of heroes and philosophers have traditionally been written by men. The woman author writes from her inner being about intimate feelings because public expression concerning other topics has always been prohibited.

However, in the last decade, the confessional novel written by women has taken a different and radical turn. It no longer presents itself in the form of young ladies' inner reflections but instead, the confessions reflect the testimonies of an entire sector of a country's population. In 1970, a key book appeared in Brazil that revolutionized the genre of confessional novels written by

Note: All quotes are based on the English translation.

women: *A Child of the Dark*, written by María Carolina de Jesús. In this novel, the author relates the story of a mother in a slum in Sao Paolo as she collects food from trash cans and searches for empty bottles to sell in order to survive. This confessional diary was followed by, *Si me permiten hablar (Let Me Speak)* by Domitila Barrios de Chungará, which recounts the accomplishments and pains of a woman in the Bolivian tin mines.

Both of these books present the other side of the coin, in that they no longer present landscapes and scenes of the protagonists' inner life, but instead reflect lives marked by pain and oppression. For this reason, it is increasingly important that this body of literature appear, be read and, above all, that the readers belong to a different group than the author. The aim of these works is to educate the world about the realities faced by the oppressed members of Latin American society.

This essay will examine another important confessional novel by a survivor, Rigoberta Menchú, a young Guatemalan woman who wrote a book that, according to the author, is that of her people. In a recent interview in Amherst, Massachusetts, Menchú said in reference to her story: "Guatemalans have worked with huipiles, which is our traditional dress, but now we are embroidering our history so that tomorrow we will be able to be weavers of huipiles again."

The book, *Me llamo Rigoberta Menchú y así me nació la conciencia* (1985) published in English as *I, Rigoberta Menchú* by Monthly Review Press is based on that tomorrow. The memoir narrates how an indigenous woman from the province of Quiché gained a sense of political consciousness through her experiences with colonization and oppression by a government that destroys the languages and beliefs of the rural people. To enter into the pages of this book is to allow oneself to become involved in the story of the humiliated and the marginal members of society: the indigenous people who form Guatemala's repressed majority. The reader witnesses the repression of Rigoberta's people, but is also exposed to their secrets and riches.

Like most of Guatemala's rural inhabitants, Rigoberta Menchú grew up speaking indigenous languages. She later learned Spanish, acquiring the language that oppressed her in order to defend herself: "I did not have the opportunity to leave my world, to dedicate myself to myself, so I began to learn Spanish three years ago" (p. 21). Rigoberta uses this language to submerge the reader in a world of magical beliefs.

Menchú speaks to us about life in her village, and about her family and their needs. She also describes the ceremony of birth, and the important link between people and the earth. This integration with nature is, according to Rigoberta, one of the essential components of her world. In talking about the values of her people, she presents a saying from her ancestors: "Our culture's customs have made us respect everything, nevertheless, we have never been respected" (p. 28).

Rigoberta's testimonies, which record her life from age eight, are full of misery and oppression. She describes how she worked on a plantation picking coffee for only 25 cents a day. Her young brother died from malnutrition on the plantation, and a friend died from pesticide poisoning. These experiences had a profound effect on Rigoberta's life and shaped her political consciousness. Throughout the book, she discusses the importance of life and the culture of life and nature, as opposed to the culture of death:

> *The act of killing a person. Death affects everyone, be it death by accident or in another way. It is something we often endure because it is something one feels in one's own flesh. For example, the way that my murdered brother died. We don't even like to kill an animal. Because we don't like to kill. There isn't violence in the indigenous community. For example, the death of a child. If a child dies from malnutrition, it isn't the parents' fault but because of the conditions created by the patrons. It is a violent act due to the system. Now they want us to live in a different way than we want to live.*

For us, killing is something monstrous. From this,
comes the indignation we feel for all the repression,
and our devotion to the struggle is related to this,
to all this suffering we feel (p. 228).

In the pages of this book, the non-violence of the indigenous people is contrasted with the violent oppression of the army that enters the land of the indigenous inhabitants and takes it from them, burns their houses, rapes their women and tortures them. Because of certain concrete experiences like the daily exploitation, and the deaths of friends and her little brother, Rigoberta joined a guerrilla group and became an organizer and defender of her people.

The memoirs of her journeys, the stories of the times she was almost captured and the account of her stay in a convent of nuns who supported the opposition forces make Rigoberta's confessions something that must be read, because the reader becomes a participant. This is the technique and most interesting merit of this type of autobiography, where the reader cannot remain undisturbed by what is told because, through the text, he or she enters into a world of human brutality and violence.

The Other Chile

Nearby flames do not resemble those sweet bonfires on the beaches at sunset. They are vengeful flames, cleverly planned with the goal of frightening and causing pain, of startling and silencing.

These flames are the visions of a bus that burns before the eyes of the passersby. No one knows if bones remain in a lost seat on what used to be a vehicle that carried passengers. A bus is burning in the pleasant city of Viña del Mar, and we watch with eyes cast down, as if we were obliged to withdraw from what we are watching and lower our heads. Under dictatorship, we have lost the ability to be shocked.

How can we be shocked when high school teachers are beheaded on a daily basis, when teenagers are burned alive and exiled. How can we maintain a sense of shock in a country fractured by fear and silence, a passivity invented by the wicked to ensure order and peace in the country.

We need shock to remove us from the mechanical inertia that lies to us, saying: "Nothing has happened here," or "I do not know anything." Right-wing dictatorships, especially the one implemented by Pinochet, have been very successful in creating an atmosphere of a fruitful and wealthy capitalism. We see shops filled with exotic clothing and expensive food. Well-dressed women display themselves on the tranquil avenues. The dictatorship veils like an elegant woman dressed in brightly-coloured frocks, her face covered by layers of make-up, masking her decaying skin.

Visitors and foreign reporters, especially North Americans, should not be fooled by the prosperity on the faces of a few Chileans. Dictatorships are skillful in instituting tombstones and castés. Those from the upper-class neighbourhoods are preoccupied with the latest fashions and the perfect tan. Members of the middle-class live in the centre of the city, and worry constantly about rent and telephone bills, invent ways to survive, to buy shoes for their children to wear to school.

This other Chile, distant and humble, resembles the slums of Lima and Rio, the ghettos of South Africa, and the barricades of an increasingly solitary Nicaragua. Life and poverty make us equal. This other Chile, with its stale smell, traces of urine and muddy paths, is hidden from view so that the other residents of Santiago do not see it, do not worry about the hunger.

To pass through this other Chile is to commune with toothless people, with lonely and squalid young prostitutes in search of a loaf of bread or a mouthful of rice for which they sell flaccid breasts and gawky legs. It is moving to see so many women alone, so many windows filled with absence. Where are the men in these marginal neighbourhoods? Many have disappeared, taken sinisterly from their homes and their children's kisses. Others, defenseless and powerless to support their families, abandon their homes and themselves in the delirium of alcoholism, to create the illusion of pains being cured and love, restored.

Then there is the hunger, that sharp pain that attacks millions of unemployed people, millions of children. The lack of nourishment is one of those incredible problems of this right-wing military dictatorship. How many children are huddled in their cribs with a cup of tea or a small bowl of broth as their only food for the day? We must point out that hunger is not just a problem in Latin America. There are 20 million malnourished individuals in the United States. Older people die from solitude and cold in this extraordinarily rich and greedy country.

Dictatorships are clever in the manipulation of images. It is very difficult for foreigners to reach the poor neighbourhoods and to speak with the people who have lost the ability to believe. The dictatorship has been skillful in creating so many different Chiles, to keeping the wealthy far from the strategies of terror. They know who to pursue. They have used the poor and humble, who fight, throw rocks, construct barricades and die, bleeding courage because they have nothing to lose.

Summer in my country. Viña del Mar seems to be teeming with sunshine and happy summer visitors. On the seemingly safe streets of this prosperous town, street vendors hawk magical rouges, rejuvenating creams and pills to bring happiness. The vendors sell things to combat hunger and the cold, to guard against the smell of war, visible yet invisible, that permeates the summer air.

Dictatorships do not pursue everyone, only the dissidents, only those who seek justice for all, only the young, only those who do not share their way of thinking. They leave the rest in peace so they will buy and dream of great, winged automobiles. Nevertheless, in Chile, when someone buys a dress, he or she is taking clothes from someone else's back, and while a woman in an upper-class neighbourhood is sunbathing, someone else is being burned with electric probes.

You sir, you ma'am, who have seen so much or have refused to see anything. What can you tell me? What should be done? What can we do before the sun sets again?

Marjorie Agosin is from Chile and is Professor of Spanish Literature at Wellesley College. She is the author of *Scraps of Life: Chilean Arpilleras* and several books of poetry. She was given the Good Neighbour Award from the National Council of Christian and Jews and also have been awarded The Distinguished Visitor Award by the Urban Morgan Institute on Human Rights College of Law, University of Cincinnati. She lives in Boston with her family.

Translator's Note

Translating the essays in this book was a wonderful learning experience, because Marjorie Agosin is a uniquely honest and inspired writer. Marjorie manages to combine personal concerns with political issues in a way that is enlightening yet never doctrinaire. In many cases, her prose is deceptively poetic, fooling the reader into focusing on the beauty of her language and images. In this way, she causes us to lower our guards and unknowingly open ourselves to the bittersweet reality she depicts, a world inhabited by women who refuse to remain silent in the face of sexism, poverty, political repression, and censorship.

Marjorie's essays are both a challenge and a pleasure to translate because her perspective and imagery are never trite or artificial. I thank her for giving me a glimpse of her world, and for entrusting me to interpret that world for an English-speaking audience.

I also thank Susan Weinstein, whose patience, suggestions, and computer contributed to this project's success.